Jesus Christ

THE ONLY SURE FOUNDATION

Jesus Christ

THE ONLY SURE FOUNDATION

AN AMALGAMATION AND REVISION OF
BY GRACE ARE WE SAVED
AND
LIFE IN CHRIST

ROBERT L. MILLET

BOOKCRAFT
SALT LAKE CITY, UTAH

Contents

Preface

$\mathcal{S}$ome things simply matter more than others. Some topics of discussion, even intellectually stimulating ones, must take a back seat to more fundamental verities. It is just so in regard to what the scriptures call the doctrine of Christ, those foundational truths associated with the person and powers of Jesus the Messiah. Who he is and what he has done are paramount and central issues; all else, however supplementary, is secondary.

This book—an amalgamation and revision of two earlier books, *By Grace Are We Saved* and *Life in Christ*—is an effort to focus attention upon certain basic realities. First, we will consider man's need for deliverance from sin and death, from that condition called "the natural man," as well as some of the futile and fruitless efforts people often make to solve their problems independent of the Master. Second, we will speak at length of the preeminence of the one perfect being to walk this earth; of his divine mission, his death and resurrection; and especially of his infinite and eternal power to renew and remake us fallible mortals. We will discuss how it is that he alone can bring to pass that quickening in the inner man that is necessary to awaken us to the things of the Spirit, and how, in the ultimate sense, he alone can wipe away our tears, bind up the brokenhearted, and declare liberty to the captives. Third, we will direct our attention toward that life which is "in Christ" and how it is we can and should build our houses of faith upon him.

Because our knowledge and understanding are cumulative, it is not always possible to identify and express specific appreciation to all those who might have helped us along the way. In the preparation of this manuscript I do owe a special debt of gratitude to Joell Woodbrey and Lori Soza, dear friends as well as conscientious secretaries and assistants, who have enthusiastically read each chapter and offered helpful suggestions. Many of my colleagues in Religious Education, other faculty members in the Philosophy, Psychology, Library Science, and Family Science departments, and numerous students at Brigham Young University—these have challenged me, encouraged me, and caused me to expand my vision and explanation of the timeless and transforming role of Jesus Christ. Though for what follows in this volume I am heavily indebted to the courteous and careful assistance of others, I alone am responsible for the conclusions drawn from the evidence cited. This book is a private endeavor and not an official publication of either The Church of Jesus Christ of Latter-day Saints or Brigham Young University.

Christ's descent below all things allowed him to ascend to celestial heights and to succor us who contend with weakness and infirmity. His life on earth, his encounter with pain and suffering, his rejection by insensitive and hostile souls, his awful agonies in Gethsemane and his unspeakable suffering on Golgotha—all these helped to perfect his empathy for the children of men (see Alma 7:11-12). Because the High Priest of our Christian profession is not an absentee Master, not a distant Deity, not one who "cannot be touched with the feeling of our infirmities"—because he too has known the perils and pains of mortality and the anguish of alienation—he knows our needs, he fully understands. Because of the intercession of Christ, we are entitled to "come boldly unto the throne of grace, that we may obtain mercy, and find grace to help in time of need." (Hebrews 4:14-16.)

The Master extends to each of us "the power of God unto salvation" (Romans 1:16), a gracious act on the part of a loving Lord. Those who ignore or spurn the proffered gift will never find the solutions to life's dilemmas and will come short of what might have been theirs in the world to come. Those who receive Christ and rely upon his mighty arm will have joy and peace here and eternal life hereafter. They come to feel the meaning and import of the Savior's declaration: "I am come that they might have life, and that they might have it more abundantly" (John 10:10).

Introduction

*S*ome years ago I sat with my counselors in a bishopric meeting. The session was drawing to a close because sacrament meeting would be starting in just ten minutes. A knock came at the door as we were making our way out of the office into the foyer. A young woman from my ward was there, who asked if she could visit with me for a moment. I indicated to her that we could chat for a bit, but that sacrament meeting would be starting soon. She assured me that we would be together for only a minute or two.

After we had been seated for a few seconds, she said: "Bishop, I need to confess a sin."

I was startled with the suddenness of the statement, but, managing to hold my composure, I offered the following: "Well, that could take some time, couldn't it? Shall we meet after the block of meetings today?"

She quickly responded: "Oh no! This will just take a second."

I nodded and asked her to go ahead, and she proceeded to describe in some detail a very serious moral transgression in which she had been involved. It was now about one minute before the meetings were to start, and so I tried again: "Why don't we get together after priesthood and Relief Society meetings."

She then staggered me with, "Well, I don't know why we would need to, unless it would be helpful to you, or something."

I indicated that such a meeting might prove beneficial to both of us. She agreed to return.

Three hours later, and after we had exchanged a few pleasantries, I asked her, "How do you feel about what has happened?"

She responded, "Just fine." I must have shown my perplexity, because she added: "For a number of hours I felt bad about what had happened, but it's okay now because I've repented."

I couldn't ask her the question fast enough, "What do you mean when you say that you have repented?" (She had explained to me earlier that the transgression had taken place on Friday night, and it was now Sunday afternoon.)

At that point, she reached into her purse, rearranged a few items, and retrieved a yellow sheet of legal-size paper. Pointing one by one to various headings that began with *R*, she said, "I've done this, and this, and this, and this, and finally I've confessed to you. I've repented."

"It seems to me that you've skipped an *R*, that your list is missing something," I said.

A startled but persistent look was in her eyes, and I noted a slight impatience with me as she said, "No, that can't be. I have everything listed here!"

"The *R* you're missing," I responded, "is *Redeemer*. You have no place for Christ on your list. I mean, what does Jesus Christ have to do with your transgression? What does what happened in Gethsemane and on Calvary some two thousand years ago have to do with what happened to you two nights ago?"

She answered: "Jesus died for me. He died for my sins."

To almost every question I asked thereafter about the Atonement she gave a perfect answer—at least, a perfectly correct answer. She had been well trained, and her answers reflected an awareness of the doctrines associated with repentance. But the answers were totally cerebral, straight from memory and mind—not from the heart. She obviously saw no real tie between her own ungodly actions and the infinite actions of a God. We spent several hours together that day and many days thereafter—searching the scriptures, praying together, and counseling over the way back to the strait and narrow path. We talked often and intently about Jesus Christ. She came in time to know the correct answers—by feeling, from the heart.

I have never been quite the same since that experience. Nor, I must add, was this the only one of its kind that I have had. Again and again I find members of the Church uncertain and aimless in their search for spiritual rest, unsure of the way to peace and happiness after serious sin. Often, very often, they, like my young ward member, have not made the vital connection between what Jesus the Christ has done for us and what we can and must now do. Such occasions as these have motivated me to search carefully the scriptures and the words of the modern prophets, to turn my heart to the Lord and seek in prayer to know and understand better finite man's relationship to an infinite Redeemer. As a result I have come to believe more strongly every day in the testimony of Nephi and have taken his words as counsel and warning for those of us who must live in a cynical and secular world, in a world that offers formulas and keys and ready access and quick fixes: "We talk of Christ," he observed, "we rejoice in Christ, we preach of Christ, we prophesy of Christ, and we write according to our prophecies, that our children may know to what source they may look for a remission of their sins" (2 Nephi 25:26).

My search of the scriptures has led me to an even deeper appreciation for our Lord and for what he has done for mankind. It has also caused me to appreciate the marvelous flood of light and intelligence that has come to us through Joseph Smith, the Book of Mormon, and modern revelation, assorted gems of priceless value that lay appropriate stress upon the goodness of our Savior, Jesus Christ, and on the concurrent obedience and faithfulness required of those who claim kinship and discipleship with him.

Perhaps one of the finest statements in all of our literature concerning the proper role of grace and works is contained in the Dictionary of the LDS Edition of the King James Bible, in which the word *grace* is defined as "a word that occurs frequently in the New Testament, especially in the writings of Paul. The main idea of the word is divine means of help or strength, given through the bounteous mercy and love of Jesus Christ." The article continues:

> It is through the grace of the Lord Jesus, made possible by his atoning sacrifice, that mankind will be raised in immortality, every person receiving his body from the grave in a condition of everlasting life. It is likewise through the grace of the Lord that individuals, through faith in the atonement of Jesus Christ and repentance of their sins, receive strength and assistance to do good works that they otherwise would not be able to maintain if left to their own means.
>
> This grace is an enabling power that allows men and women to lay hold on eternal life and exaltation after they have expended their own best efforts.
>
> Divine grace is needed by every soul in consequence of the fall of Adam and also because of man's weaknesses and shortcomings. However, grace cannot suffice without total effort on the part of the recip-

ient. Hence the explanation, "It is by grace that we are saved, after all we can do" (2 Nephi 25:23). It is truly the grace of Jesus Christ that makes salvation possible.[1]

As with so many others, "I stand all amazed at the love Jesus offers me, confused at the grace that so fully he proffers me."[2] I have no hesitation and feel no shame in acknowledging that I do not understand the particulars of how the atonement of Christ was brought to pass, how it was that Jesus of Nazareth assumed the burden of the sins of mankind. I do know, however, that it has been accomplished, and that even though for the time being it is inexplicable to finite minds, we can take full advantage of the gifts of God so readily available through him who is mighty to save.

I know that because of the tender regard and selfless sacrifice of that one being, "unto every one of us is given grace according to the measure of the gift of Christ" (Ephesians 4:7). Like Nephi, "I glory in [this] truth. I glory in my Jesus, for he hath redeemed my soul from hell" (2 Nephi 33:6). "For the grace of God which bringeth salvation to all men, hath appeared; teaching us that, denying ungodliness and worldly lusts, we should live soberly, righteously, and godly, in this present world; looking for that blessed hope, and the glorious appearing of the great God and our Savior Jesus Christ; who gave himself for us, that he might redeem us from all iniquity, and purify unto himself a peculiar people, zealous of good works" (JST, Titus 2:11-14).

Notes

1. LDS Bible Dictionary, s.v. "Grace," p. 697.
2. *Hymns,* no. 193.

The way is prepared from the fall of man,
and salvation is free.
—2 Nephi 2:4

1

Salvation Is Free

*S*alvation, which is exaltation, which is eternal life, is free. It is not something for which we can barter, nor something that may be purchased with money. Nor in the strictest sense is it something that may be *earned*. More correctly, salvation is a gift, a gift most precious, something gloriously transcendent that may only be *inherited*. "If thou wilt do good," the Lord explained to Oliver Cowdery, "yea, and hold out faithful to the end, thou shalt be saved in the kingdom of God, which is the greatest of all the gifts of God; for there is no gift greater than the gift of salvation" (D&C 6:13). To David Whitmer that same Lord affirmed: "If you keep my commandments and endure to the end you shall have eternal life, which gift is the greatest of all the gifts of God" (D&C 14:7).

In commending his son Jacob on the manner in which he had learned wisdom and followed righteousness in his youth, Lehi said: "Thou hast beheld in thy youth his [Christ's] glory; wherefore, thou art blessed even as they unto whom he shall minister in the flesh; for the Spirit is the same, yesterday, today, and forever. And *the way is prepared from the fall of man, and salvation is free.*" (2 Nephi 2:4, italics added.) Indeed, salvation is free, freely available, freely to be found by those who seek and inquire and obey. When the prophets who lived before the coming of our Lord in the flesh spoke of salvation being free, they were in effect declaring the same doctrine that would flow from the lips and pens of Apostles and prophets in the statement that we are saved by the grace of Christ. That is to say, free salvation is salvation by grace.

"The questions then are: What salvation is free? What salvation comes by the grace of God? With all the emphasis of the rolling thunders of Sinai, we answer: All salvation is free; all comes by the merits and mercy and grace of the Holy Messiah; there is no salvation of any kind, nature, or degree that is not bound to Christ and his atonement."[1]

In the words of Isaiah and Nephi, the people of the earth are summoned to come to the waters of life, to acquire the milk and honey of the gospel, but to do so without money and without price. "Hath [the Lord] commanded any that they should not partake of his salvation?" Nephi asked. "Nay," he answered, "but he hath given it free for all men. . . . Behold, hath the Lord commanded any that they should not partake of his goodness? Behold I say unto you, Nay; but all men are privileged the one like unto the other, and none are forbidden." (2 Nephi 26:25-28.)

A Gospel of Grace

In our efforts to stress the importance of good works—of receiving the ordinances of salvation, of living by every word of God, of standing as witnesses of Christ at all times, and of involving ourselves in the acts of Christian service that always characterize the disciples of Jesus in any age—we are sometimes wont to overlook the simple yet profound reality that the plan of salvation, the gospel of Jesus Christ, is truly a gospel of grace. "Does salvation come by grace, by grace alone," Elder Bruce R. McConkie asked, "by grace without works? It surely does," he answered, "without any question, in all its parts, types, kinds, and degrees."

> We are saved by grace, without works; it is a gift of God. How else could it come?
>
> In his goodness and grace the great God ordained and established the plan of salvation. No works on our part were required.
>
> In his goodness and grace he created this earth and all that is on it, with man as the crowning creature of his creating—without which creation his spirit children could not obtain immortality and eternal life. No works on our part were required.

In his goodness and grace he provided for the Fall of man, thus bringing mortality and death and a probationary estate into being—without all of which there would be no immortality and eternal life. And again no works on our part were required.

In his goodness and grace—and this above all—he gave his Only Begotten Son to ransom man and all life from the temporal and spiritual death brought into the world by the Fall of Adam. . . .

There is nothing any man could do to create himself. This was the work of the Lord God.

Nor did we have any part in the Fall of man, without which there could be no salvation. The Lord provided the way, and Adam and Eve put the system into operation.

And finally, there neither has been, nor is, nor ever can be any way nor means by which man alone can, by any power he possesses, redeem himself.[2]

More specifically, through the atonement of Christ there are numerous blessings which accrue to mortal man, these coming as unconditional benefits of the work of redemption, acts of pure grace.

Had there been no atonement, because of the fall of our first parents this earth and all forms of life upon it would have been shut out forever from the presence of the Eternal God; man would have been severed completely from the regenerating powers of the Spirit. But because of the love and condescensions and mercies of the Holy One, the light and life of Christ are extended to earth and its inhabitants, "otherwise [we] could not abound" (D&C 88:49-50; compare 11:28; 39:1-3; Mosiah 2:21).

Second, agency and moral freedom are made available to all through the Atonement. "The Messiah cometh in the fulness of time," Lehi taught, "that he may redeem the children of men from the fall. And because that they are redeemed from the fall they have become free forever, knowing good from evil; to act for themselves and not to be acted upon. . . . They are free to choose liberty and eternal life, through the great Mediator of all men, or to choose captivity and death, according to the captivity and power of the devil." (2 Nephi 2:26-27; compare 10:23; Helaman 14:30.) People in all ages are thus able to stand fast "in the liberty wherewith Christ hath made us free" (Galatians 5:1).

Third, those who live and die without gospel law or without understanding or accountability are not subject to the demands of

God's justice. Jacob explained therefore that in cases "where there is no condemnation, the mercies of the Holy One of Israel have claim upon them, because of the atonement" (2 Nephi 9:25-26). Benjamin likewise taught his people that the blood of Christ atones "for the sins of those who have fallen by the transgression of Adam, who have died not knowing the will of God concerning them, or who have ignorantly sinned" (Mosiah 3:11; compare 15:24; Moroni 8:22). This principle and benefit applies to little children who die before the time of accountability: they remain innocent before the Lord and are not subject to the tempter's power; they are assured of eternal life (see Moses 6:53-54; Moroni 8; D&C 29:46-48; 93:38-42).

Finally, because of the ransoming power and the intercessory role of Jesus Christ, all men and women will follow the pattern of their Risen Lord as to the resurrection: they will receive the free gift of immortality—they will be raised from the dead in the resurrection to inherit a physical body. "For since by man came death, by man came also the resurrection of the dead. For as in Adam all die, even so in Christ shall all be made alive." (1 Corinthians 15:21-22.) When the time has fully come and the trump is sounded, "then shall all the dead awake, for their graves shall be opened, and they shall come forth—yea, even all" (D&C 29:26; compare Alma 11:40-44). No works or labors or mortal deeds are necessary to bring these eventualities to pass; they come from a gracious Lord who desires to save all of the children of the Father.

Truly we are the recipients of graces without number, are beneficiaries of the Lord's love and condescensions, of gifts that are beyond our power to work for, earn, or even adequately express gratitude for. As we shall see presently, in order to gain eternal life men and women must demonstrate, through faithful living, a genuine receipt of the Atonement and the plan of salvation: they must keep the commandments and evidence their fidelity and devotion to the Lord and his work in order to accept these precious gifts. "If we walk in the light, as he is in the light, we have fellowship one with another, and the blood of Jesus Christ his Son cleanseth us from all sin" (1 John 1:7). But such works of man, no matter what their quantity or quality, in no way alter the fact that we are saved by the grace of Christ—by and through unearned divine assistance. Like Nephi, we joy in the covenants of the Lord, we delight "in his grace, and in his justice, and power, and mercy in the great and eternal plan of deliverance from death" (2 Nephi 11:5).

Notes

1. Bruce R. McConkie, *The Promised Messiah* (Salt Lake City: Deseret Book Co., 1978), pp. 346-47.

2. "What Think Ye of Salvation by Grace?" *1983-84 Fireside and Devotional Speeches* (Provo, Utah: Brigham Young University Press, 1984), p. 47.

2

Enemies to God

*T*he gospel, or plan of salvation, is designed, according to President Brigham Young, for "the redemption of fallen beings."[1] That there is a plan of deliverance implies that there must be something from which we need deliverance. This is a hard doctrine, one from which too many Latter-day Saints have sought to hide. But it strikes at the heart and core of revealed religion. We must beware of temporizing doctrines that would soften the effects of the Fall and thus diminish the necessity for the Atonement. The Fall is a companion doctrine with the Atonement, and I am not acquainted with any serious or extended treatment of the Atonement in the Book of Mormon, for example, that is not somehow connected—directly or by obvious implication—with the Fall.

The Doctrine of the Fall

We know that Adam and Eve partook of the forbidden fruit. They transgressed. They were cast from the Garden of Eden and from the presence of the Lord. Then came blood and sweat and toil and opposition and bodily decay and finally death. Even though the Fall was a vital part of the great plan of the Eternal God—as much a foreappointed event as Christ's intercession—as a result of it man's state, including his relationship to and contact with God, changed dramatically. Early in the Nephite record it is recorded that Lehi "spake concerning the prophets, how great a number had testified of . . . [the] Redeemer of the world. Wherefore, all mankind were in a lost and in a fallen state, and ever would be save they should rely on this Redeemer." (1 Nephi 10:5-6.) Again, man's need for redemption is presupposed by the coming of a Messiah.

Joseph Smith wrote to John Wentworth: "We believe that men will be punished for their own sins, and not for Adam's transgression" (Articles of Faith 1:2). This proclamation is in effect affirmed in the Lord's statement to Adam: "I have forgiven thee thy transgression in the Garden of Eden" (Moses 6:53). This declaration has, unfortunately, been misunderstood. Even though God forgave our first parents their transgression; even though there is no "original sin" entailed upon Adam and Eve's children; even though "the Son of God hath atoned for original guilt, wherein the sins of the parents cannot be answered upon the heads of the children" (Moses 6:54)—despite this clear absence of guilt for our first parents' transgression, we must not conclude that all is well, that the Fall has no effect upon us.

To say that man is not under sin is not to say that man is untainted or unaffected. Jehovah explained to Adam: "*Inasmuch as thy children are conceived in sin, even so when they begin to grow up, sin conceiveth in their hearts,* and they taste the bitter, that they may know to prize the good" (Moses 6:55, italics added). No, of course we do not believe, with Calvin, in the moral depravity of men and women. No, we do not believe, with Luther, that man, because of his carnality and depravity, does not even have the power to choose good over evil. And we do not believe that children are born in sin, that they inherit the so-called sin of Adam either through sexual union or by birth. Rather, children are *conceived* in sin: meaning first, that they are conceived into a world of sin, and second, that conception is the vehicle by which the effects of the Fall (not the original transgression, which God has forgiven) are transmitted to Adam's posterity.

To say that we are not punished for their transgression is not to say that we are unaffected by it. Lehi taught Jacob that in the beginning God "gave commandment that all men must repent; for he showed unto all men that they were lost, because of the transgression of their parents" (2 Nephi 2:21). Thus we all have need to repent, since all have the ability, the propensity, to sin because all inherit Adam's fallen nature. "We know that thou art holy," the brother of Jared confessed to the Lord, "and dwellest in the heavens, and that we are unworthy before thee; *because of the fall our natures have become evil continually;* nevertheless, O Lord, thou hast given us a commandment that we must call upon thee, that from thee we may receive according to our desires" (Ether 3:2, italics added). Again, conception is the mechanism of transmission, the means by which Adam's fallen nature is passed on to his children and thereby from generation to generation. Thus sin is implanted in man's nature at conception, just as death is implanted at the same time. Both of these—death and sin—are present only in seed form at conception, and therefore a child is neither dead nor sinful when born. Death and sin do, however, come to pass as a result of man's nature as he grows up. Sin comes naturally, just as does death.

The testimony of ancient Book of Mormon prophets is confirmed by the teachings of modern Apostles and prophets. Elder Bruce R. McConkie summarized the effects of the Fall as follows:

> Adam fell. We know that this fall came because of transgression, and that Adam broke the law of God, became mortal, and was thus subject to sin and disease and all the ills of mortality. We know that the effects of his fall passed upon all his posterity; all inherited a fallen state, a state of mortality, a state in which spiritual and temporal death prevail. In this state all men sin. All are lost. All are fallen. All are cut off from the presence of God. . . . Such a way of life is inherent in this mortal existence. . . .
>
> Death entered the world by means of Adam's fall—death of two kinds, temporal and spiritual. Temporal death passes upon all men when they depart this mortal life. It is then that the eternal spirit steps out of its earthly tenement, to take up an abode in a realm where spirits are assigned, to await the day of their resurrection. *Spiritual death passes upon all men when they become accountable for their sins. Being thus subject to sin they die spiritually;* they die as pertaining to the things of the Spirit; they die as pertaining to the things of righteousness; they are cast out of the presence of God. It is of such men that the scriptures speak when they say that the natural man is an enemy to God.[2]

"I have learned in my travels," Joseph Smith the Prophet observed, "that man is treacherous and selfish, but few excepted."[3] "Men have ever been prone to apostasy," President John Taylor pointed out. "Our fallen nature is at enmity with a godly life."[4]

The Natural Man

King Benjamin said that those who sin against light, who "go contrary to that which has been spoken," withdraw themselves from the directing influence and power of the Spirit of the Lord. "I say unto you," he continued, "that the man that doeth this, the same cometh out in open rebellion against God; therefore he listeth to obey the evil spirit, and becometh an enemy to all righteousness; therefore, the Lord has no place in him, for he dwelleth not in unholy temples" (Mosiah 2:36-37). Benjamin later explained: "The natural man is an enemy to God, and has been from the fall of Adam, and will be, forever and ever, unless he yields to the enticings of the Holy Spirit, and putteth off the natural man and becometh a saint through the atonement of Christ the Lord" (Mosiah 3:19).

What is it that King Benjamin is saying about mankind? What is the natural man, and how may he or she be characterized?

Simply stated, the natural man is the unregenerated man, the man who remains in his fallen condition, who lives without God and godliness in the world. He is the unredeemed man, a person uninfluenced by the light of Christ, a being who lives by his own light. Frequently the natural man is a person bent on lechery and lasciviousness; he may be one who loves Satan more than God and thereby is carnal, sensual, and devilish (Moses 5:13). After having preached and pleaded with his son Corianton and testified that wickedness never was happiness, Alma said: "And now, my son, all men that are in a state of nature, or I would say, in a carnal state, are in the gall of bitterness and in the bonds of iniquity." Now note how it is that such persons are enemies to God: "They are without God in the world, and they have gone contrary to the nature of God; therefore, they are in a state contrary to the nature of happiness." (Alma 41:10-11.)

In the same vein, just prior to his martyrdom Abinadi warned the priests of Noah of that day wherein natural men—in this case the vile and wicked—would receive their just rewards: "And then shall the wicked be cast out, and they shall have cause to howl, and weep, and wail, and gnash their teeth; and this because they would not hearken to the voice of the Lord; therefore the Lord redeemeth them not. For they are carnal and devilish, and the devil has power over them; yea, even that old serpent that did beguile our first parents, which was the cause of their fall."

Then Abinadi explained how the Fall opened the way for men and women to reject the Spirit and choose sin: "Which [fall] was the cause of all mankind becoming carnal, sensual, devilish, knowing evil from good, subjecting themselves to the devil. Thus all mankind were lost; and behold they would have been endlessly lost were it not that God redeemed his people from their lost and fallen state."

At this point one might be prone to sit back, let out a sigh of relief, and offer gratitude to God that because of the atoning work of Christ the battle is over. But Abinadi continued his warning: "Remember that he that persists in his own carnal nature, and goes on in the ways of sin and rebellion against God, remaineth in his fallen state and the devil hath all power over him. Therefore he is as though there was no redemption made, being an enemy to God; and also is the devil an enemy to God." (Mosiah 16:2-5.) We should here attend carefully to the fact that the phrase "persists in his own carnal nature" implies that individuals have such a nature to persist in, this in spite of the Atonement. Further, "remaineth in his fallen state" does not simply mean *get into* a fallen state through sin.

On the other hand, the natural man need not be what we would call degenerate. He may well be a "nice man," a moral and upright woman, one bent upon goodness and benevolence. However, he or she operates in and is acclimated to the present fallen world. Such a person does not enjoy the enlivening powers of the Holy Ghost: he has not received the revealed witness of the truth and has not enjoyed the sanctifying powers of the blood of Christ. Though proper and appropriate in regard to societal standards, he has not responded sufficiently to the Light of Christ to be led to the covenant gospel (Mosiah 16:2; D&C 84:46-48). "The whole world lieth in sin," the Savior declared in a modern revelation, "and groaneth under darkness and under the bondage of sin. And by this you may know they are under the bondage of sin, because they come not unto me." (D&C 84:49-50.) More specifically, in regard to those outside the restored gospel, "There are none that doeth good except those who are ready to receive the fulness of my gospel, which I have sent forth unto this generation" (D&C 35:12).

And what of members of The Church of Jesus Christ of Latter-day Saints? Are any of us "natural men"? We certainly qualify for that horrid title if we are guilty of gross wickedness, if we have sinned against gospel light and not thoroughly repented. And yes, we are guilty too if we persist in a nature that leads us to exist in twilight when we might bask in the light of the Son. President Brigham Young exhorted the people of the Church in 1867: "There is no doubt, if a person lives according to the revelations given to God's people, he may have the Spirit of the Lord to signify to him His will, and to guide and to direct him in the discharge of his duties, in his temporal as well as his spiritual exercises. I am satisfied, however, that in this respect, we live far beneath our privileges."[5] Members of the Church who refuse to climb toward greater spiritual heights, who have no inclination to reach down and further anchor themselves in the truth, who have become satisfied with their present spiritual state—these are they who are natural men, persons generally of good will who do not understand that through their smugness and complacency they are aiding and abetting the cause of the enemy of all righteousness. "Fallen man," C. S. Lewis perceptively observed, "is not simply an imperfect creature who needs improvement: he is a rebel who must lay down his arms."[6]

What are some broad characteristics of natural men? Consider the following:

1. *Natural men are unable or unwilling to perceive spiritual realities.* Paul explained that "the natural man receiveth not the things of the Spirit of God: for they are foolishness unto him: neither can he know them, because they are spiritually discerned" (1 Corinthians 2:14). In exulting over the Lord's infinite mercy—in his willingness to snatch his children from evil and forgive their sins—Ammon said: "What natural man is there that knoweth these things? I say unto you, there is none that knoweth these things, save it be the penitent." (Alma 26:21.) "No man has seen God at any time in the flesh, except quickened by the Spirit of God," a modern revelation teaches. "Neither can any natural man abide the presence of God, neither after the carnal mind." (D&C 67:11-12; compare Moses 1:11.) "How difficult it is to teach the natural man," Brigham Young declared, "who comprehends nothing more than that which he sees with the natural eye!" He continued:

> How hard it is for him to believe! How difficult would be the task to make the philosopher, who, for many years, has argued himself into the belief that his spirit is no more after his body sleeps in the grave, believe that his intelligence came from eternity, and is as eternal, in its

nature, as the elements, or as the Gods. Such doctrine by him would be considered vanity and foolishness, it would be entirely beyond his comprehension. It is difficult, indeed, to remove an opinion or belief into which he has argued himself from the mind of the natural man. Talk to him about angels, heavens, God, immortality, and eternal lives, and it is like sounding brass, or a tinkling cymbal to his ears; it has no music to him; there is nothing in it that charms his senses, soothes his feelings, attracts his attention, or engages his affections, in the least; to him it is all vanity.[7]

2. *Natural men are fiercely independent.* Joseph Smith taught that "all men are naturally disposed to walk in their own paths as they are pointed out by their own fingers, and are not willing to consider and walk in the path which is pointed out by another, saying, This is the way, walk ye in it, although he should be an unerring director, and the Lord his God sent him."[8] Seeking to "be his own man," the natural man actually ends up (ironically) conforming to the trends of the day. C. S. Lewis remarked that "until you have given up your self to [the Lord] you will not have a real self. Sameness is to be found most among the most 'natural' men, not among those who surrender to Christ. How monotonously alike all the great tyrants and conquerors have been: how gloriously different are the saints."[9]

Samuel the Lamanite expressed the tragic end of those whose natural view of reality causes them to spend their days climbing the wrong ladder: "But behold, your days of probation are past; ye have procrastinated the day of your salvation until it is everlastingly too late, and your destruction is made sure; yea, for ye have sought all the days of your lives for that which ye could not obtain; and ye have sought for happiness in doing iniquity, which thing is contrary to the nature of that righteousness which is in our great and Eternal Head" (Helaman 13:38). In the words of a Protestant counselor: "Fallen man has taken command of his own life, determined above all else to prove that he's adequate for the job. And like the teen who feels rich until he starts paying for his own car insurance, we remain confident of our ability to manage life until we face the reality of our own soul. . . . To put it simply, people want to run their own lives. Fallen man is both terrified of vulnerability and committed to maintaining independence. . . . The most natural thing for us to do is to develop strategies for finding life that reflect our commitment to depending on our own resources."[10]

3. *Natural men are proud, overly competitive, reactionary, and externally driven.* The natural man—be he the irreverent and ungodly or the well-meaning and the spiritually stillborn—is preoccupied with self and obsessed with personal aggrandizement. His life is keyed to the rewards of this ephemeral sphere, his values derived solely from pragmatism and utility. He takes his cues from the world and the worldly.

The central feature of pride, as President Ezra Taft Benson warned the Latter-day Saints, is enmity—enmity toward God and enmity toward man. The look of the natural man is neither up (to God) nor over (to man), except as the horizontal glance allows him to maintain a distance from his fellows. "Pride is essentially competitive in nature," President Benson explained. "We pit our will against God's. When we direct our pride toward God, it is in the spirit of 'my will and not thine be done.'. . . The proud cannot accept the authority of God giving directions to their lives. . . . The proud wish God would agree with them. They aren't interested in changing their opinions to agree with God's." In relation to their fellowmen, these "are tempted daily to elevate [themselves] above others and diminish them." For the proud, as President Benson quoted from C. S. Lewis's *Mere Christianity,* there is no pleasure in "having something," only in "having more of it than the next man." In short, said President Benson, "pride is the universal sin, the great vice." Further, "pride is the great stumbling block to Zion."[11]

4. *Natural men yield themselves to the harsh and the crude.* The Spirit of the Lord has a calming and quieting influence upon those who cultivate it and enjoy its fruits. As a sanctifier, the Holy Ghost "expands and purifies all the natural passions and affections. . . . It inspires virtue, kindness, goodness, tenderness, gentleness and charity."[12] On the other hand, as President Spencer W. Kimball declared, the natural man—the man who lives without this divine refinement—"is the 'earthy man' who has allowed rude animal passions to overshadow his spiritual inclinations."[13] Rudeness characterizes such a man's relationships, crudeness such a woman's speech and manner.

Frequent Reactions to the Doctrine

We should here observe that reactions to the doctrine that the natural man is an enemy of God are numerous. Some of these we will now consider.

1. *All men enjoy the Light of Christ.* A first reaction to this doctrine is that every person that comes into the world is endowed with the Light of Christ. The truth of the matter is that the Light of Christ is a gift and endowment from God. That is, to be spiritually effective the Spirit of Jesus Christ must be received by the spirit of man. From the natural or external perspective, it is true that the Light of Christ comes to us as physical light, that it brings order and provides law for all existence in heaven and on earth. Literally, without it we could not exist or abound (D&C 88:6-13, 50). From an inner or redemptive perspective, however, the Light of Christ must be received—it must be accepted, heeded—in order for a person to be enlightened and thereafter redeemed from the fallen state. Because man has his agency, he can choose to accept or reject this light. Whether such redemptive light takes the form of reason or judgment or conscience, we must exercise faith in order to enjoy its full benefits (D&C 84:42-50). Thus, although it is true that the Spirit gives light to all men (naturally), that Light enlightens only those who heed it (redemptively).

2. *The spirit of man is good.* Some who contend that man is basically good, that his inherent inclination is to choose righteousness, enjoy quoting a statement from President Brigham Young in which he seems to take quite a different view of who and what the natural man is.

> It is fully proved in all the revelations that God has ever given to mankind that they naturally love and admire righteousness, justice and truth more than they do evil. It is, however, universally received by professors of religion as a scriptural doctrine that man is naturally opposed to God. This is not so. Paul says, in his Epistle to the Corinthians, "But the natural man receiveth not the things of God," but I say it is the unnatural "man that receiveth not the things of God." . . . That which was, is, and will continue to endure is more natural than that which will pass away and be no more. The natural man is of God.[14]

In light of a belief in human depravity held by so many in the nineteenth century, there is no question but that the doctrines of the Restoration were as a refreshing breeze in a dry and arid spiritual climate. The revealed word that God had forgiven Adam's transgression, as well as the corollary principle that little children who die before the age of accountability are saved—these beliefs served to set the Latter-day Saints apart from much of the Christian world and certainly painted a more positive and optimistic picture in regard to the nature of man. It is our belief that we lived before we came here, that we are all the sons and daughters of God, and that our spirits literally inherited from our exalted sire the capacity to eventually be like him. These are all true doctrines. When understood, they can do much to lift the sights of man toward the glorious and the ennobling.

Such beliefs, however, do not invalidate the burden of scripture—that there was a fall, and that that fall takes a measured and meaningful toll upon earth's inhabitants. Obviously President Young is using the phrase "natural man" differently than Benjamin or Paul. His reference is to the spirit of man, the willing and striving eternal agent that is a child of God. His point is a good one: man can choose good as well as evil; can, through the proper exercise of his God-given agency, become a spiritual being before the Almighty. And yet the spirit can be and is influenced by the physical body, inasmuch as the latter is subject to our present fallen state. President Young taught:

> Now, I want to tell you that [Satan] does not hold any power over man, only so far as the body overcomes the spirit that is in a man, through yielding to the spirit of evil. The spirit that the Lord puts into a tabernacle of flesh is under the dictation of the Lord Almighty; but the spirit and body are united in order that the spirit may have a tabernacle, and be exalted; and the spirit is influenced by the body, and the body by the spirit. In the first place the spirit is pure, and under the special control and influence of the Lord, but the body is of the earth, and is subject to the power of the devil, and is under the mighty influence of that fallen nature that is of the earth. If the spirit yields to the body, the devil then has power to overcome both the body and spirit of that man.[15]

On another occasion, President Young taught that "there are no persons without evil passions to embitter their lives. Mankind are revengeful, passionate, hateful, and devilish in their dispositions. This we inherit through the fall, and the grace of God is designed to enable us to overcome it."[16]

3. *Little children are innocent.* Too often Latter-day Saints—concerned about and confused over the scriptural statement that children

are conceived in sin (Moses 6:55)—ask the question, Are children pure? The answer to this question is always a resounding yes. No Latter-day Saint disputes that. The real issue is *why* children are pure. Two answers suggest themselves: (1) The Greek or humanistic response is that children are pure because human nature is pure, prone toward the good; and (2) the Christian response is that children are pure because of the Atonement, because Jesus Christ has declared them so. Children are redeemed because of the righteousness of our Redeemer. Benjamin, presumably still quoting the angel, said: "And even if it were possible that little children could sin they could not be saved." That is, if Christ required children to be responsible for those actions or deeds that are ostensibly wrong and sinful, they could not be saved had there been no atonement. "But I say unto you they are blessed; for behold, *as in Adam, or by nature, they fall, even so the blood of Christ atoneth for their sins.*" (Mosiah 3:16, italics added.)

The revelations state that little children "cannot sin, for power is not given unto Satan to tempt little children, until they begin to become accountable before me" (D&C 29:47). All of us know of deeds performed by little children that may only be described as evil. I am aware of a seven-year-old who in an act of rage killed his brother. The act of murder is a heinous sin. But in this case the child's action is not accounted as sin. Why? Because, in the words of God, "little children are redeemed from the foundation of the world through mine Only Begotten" (D&C 29:46). Christ explained through Mormon that "the curse of Adam is taken from [children] in me, that it hath no power over them" (Moroni 8:8). Little children are subject to the pull and effects of the Fall, just as everyone is. They are not, however, held accountable for their acts. In summary, little children are saved without any preconditions—without faith, repentance, or baptism. Their innocence is decreed and declared by and through the tender mercies of an all-loving Lord. They are innocent through the Atonement.

Conclusion

We shall spend all our days seeking to subdue the flesh and put off the natural man; this is the challenge of mortality. "Will sin be perfectly destroyed?" Brigham Young asked. "No, it will not, for it is not so designed in the economy of Heaven." He went on:

> Do not suppose that we shall ever in the flesh be free from temptations to sin. Some suppose that they can in the flesh be sanctified body and spirit and become so pure that they will never again feel the effects of the power of the adversary of truth. Were it possible for a person to attain to this degree of perfection in the flesh, he could not die neither remain in a world where sin predominates. Sin has entered into the world, and death by sin. I think we shall more or less feel the effects of sin so long as we live, and finally have to pass the ordeals of death.[17]

Just as no person desires food until he has hunger, so the living waters can bless our lives only to the degree that we acknowledge our fallen condition, seek diligently to put off the natural man, and receive through repentance deliverance from sin. "It requires all the atonement of Christ," President Young pointed out, "the mercy of the Father, the pity of angels and the grace of the Lord Jesus Christ to be with us always, and then to do the very best we possibly can, to get rid of this sin within us, so that we may escape from this world into the celestial kingdom." [18]

Notes

1. In *Journal of Discourses*, 26 vols. (Liverpool: F. D. Richards & Sons, 1855-86), 1:1.

2. *The Promised Messiah* (Salt Lake City: Deseret Book Co., 1978), pp. 244, 349-50, italics added.

3. *Teachings of the Prophet Joseph Smith,* sel. Joseph Fielding Smith (Salt Lake City: Deseret Book, 1976), p. 30.

4. *The Mediation and Atonement of our Lord and Savior Jesus Christ* (Salt Lake City: Deseret News Co., 1882), 1972 lithographic reprint, p. 197.

5. In *Journal of Discourses* 12:104.

6. *Mere Christianity* (New York: Macmillan Publishing Company, 1960), p. 59.

7. In *Journal of Discourses* 1:2.

8. *Teachings of the Prophet Joseph Smith*, pp. 26-27.

9. *Mere Christianity*, p. 190.

10. Larry Crabb, *Inside Out* (Colorado Springs: NavPress, 1988), pp. 15-16, 54.

11. In Conference Report, April 1989, pp. 3-7.

12. Parley P. Pratt, *Key to the Science of Theology* (Salt Lake City: Deseret Book Co., 1978), p. 61.

13. In Conference Report, October 1974, p. 161.

14. In *Journal of Discourses* 9:305.

15. In *Journal of Discourses* 2:255-56.

16. In *Journal of Discourses* 8:160.

17. In *Journal of Discourses* 10:173.

18. In *Journal of Discourses* 11:301.

Cursed is he that putteth his trust in
man or maketh flesh his arm.
—2 Nephi 4:34

3

Broken Cisterns

$\mathcal{O}$ne of the tragic ironies of our day is that so many are dying of thirst while the cooling waters of life are within reach. Some are not aware that deliverance is available. Others, sad to say, are not even aware that they thirst.

The Lord Jehovah, speaking anciently through Jeremiah, said: "My people have committed two evils; they have forsaken me the fountain of living waters, and hewed them out cisterns, broken cisterns, that can hold no water" (Jeremiah 2:13). In summarizing this statement, we note first that most of the earth's inhabitants have forsaken the Lord. Second, all people thirst, even if they are unaware of their needs. Finally, most people pursue their quest for the living water inappropriately—they choose alternate paths, often irresponsible and usually unproductive and empty strategies. The world may have its agenda; the Savior usually has another approach entirely. There is safety and security only in discovering and implementing the Lord's way.

The Arm of Flesh

Isaiah aptly described the human inclination and the consequent plight of mankind: "All we like sheep have gone astray; we have turned every one to his own way" (Isaiah 53:6). One of the evidences of the Fall is the manner in which natural men work intently against their own best interest. Being blind to spiritual realities—to things as they really are—men and women trust in their own strength and rely on their own unaided and unenlightened perspective. The Lord said of man in Isaiah's day, "I have spread out my hands all the day unto a rebellious people, which walketh in a way that was not good, after their own thoughts" (Isaiah 65:2).

Of the world at the time of the Restoration—and surely in regard to people today and in the future—Christ declared: "They seek not the Lord to establish his righteousness, but every man walketh in his own way, and after the image of his own god, whose image is in the likeness of the world, and whose substance is that of an idol, which waxeth old and shall perish in Babylon, even Babylon the great, which shall fall."

It was because of this—because the people on earth had been wandering in darkness as a result of trusting in the arm of flesh—that the heavens were rent in the spring of 1820. "Wherefore, I the Lord, knowing the calamity which should come upon the inhabitants of the earth, called upon my servant Joseph Smith, Jun., and spake unto him from heaven, and gave him commandments." That is to say, because the world was turned inward; because men and women had placed their ultimate trust in men and women; because such actions and attitudes constitute idolatry and lead to spiritual impotence and apostasy from the truth—because of these dire conditions God raised up Joseph Smith and reestablished his everlasting covenant on earth. Thus what the worldly would call "the weak things of the world shall come forth and break down [what the myopic would call] the mighty and strong ones, that man should not counsel his fellow man, neither trust in the arm of flesh." (D&C 1:16-17, 19.)

There is no sin in trusting man, so long as one's ultimate reliance is on the Lord. God is offended when we ignore or reject inspired counsel in favor of social approval and acceptance, when we "trust in the arm of flesh."

> Thus saith the Lord; Cursed be the man that trusteth in man, and maketh flesh his arm, and whose heart departeth from the Lord.
>
> For he shall be like the heath [juniper tree] in the desert, and shall not see when good cometh; but shall inhabit the parched places in the wilderness, in a salt land and not inhabited.
>
> Blessed is the man that trusteth in the Lord, and whose hope the Lord is.

For he shall be as a tree planted by the waters, and that spreadeth out her roots by the river, and shall not see [fear] when heat cometh, but her leaf shall be green. (Jeremiah 17:5-8.)

Nephi exulted in his Maker: "O Lord, I have trusted in thee, and I will trust in thee forever. I will not put my trust in the arm of flesh; for I know that cursed is he that putteth his trust in the arm of flesh. Yea, cursed is he that putteth his trust in man or maketh flesh his arm." (2 Nephi 4:34.)

In one sense, trusting in the arm of flesh borders on false worship; it partakes of the spirit of idolatry. President Spencer W. Kimball explained:

Few men have ever knowingly and deliberately chosen to reject God and his blessings. Rather, we learn from the scriptures that because the exercise of faith has always appeared to be more difficult than relying on things more immediately at hand, carnal man has tended to transfer his trust in God to material things. Therefore, in all ages when men have fallen under the power of Satan and lost the faith, they have put in its place a hope in the "arm of flesh" and in "gods of silver, and gold, of brass, iron, wood, and stone, which see not, nor hear, nor know" (Daniel 5:23)—that is, in idols. This I find to be a dominant theme in the Old Testament. Whatever thing a man sets his heart and his trust in most is his god; and if his god doesn't also happen to be the true and living God of Israel, that man is laboring in idolatry.[1]

It is not simply the love of wealth or the quest for fame of which the scriptures and prophets warn us. Jesus reminded us that in the last days there would arise "false Christs" and false prophets. There are always a few deluded and misguided individuals who claim to be Jesus or who believe themselves to be divine. The prophetic warning about false Christs, however, seldom refers to such eccentrics. Rather, false Christs are false religions, false systems of salvation. They are individuals or organizations who offer salvation or deliverance from sin on some basis—any basis—other than that which God has established through authorized channels. In the end, of course, they simply cannot deliver. They are either woefully deficient or inexcusably perverse.

There are also false programs, false educational ideas that offer relief from the stress and pulls of the world, but have not the means nor the power to deliver what they promise. With a vision of our day before him, Nephi spoke: "They have all gone astray save it be a few, who are the humble followers of Christ; nevertheless, they are led, that in many instances they do err because they are taught by the precepts of men" (2 Nephi 28:14). This is a sobering warning. Faithful members of the Church have in many instances been deceived, their faith weakened, and their discipleship diluted through the mingling of scripture with the philosophies of men. The marriage of Zion and Babylon is an unholy union; it is a vain attempt to harmonize and integrate disparate kingdoms. In the quest for peace between warring ideologies, gospel principles are compromised and costly concessions made.

We live in a day when the religious solutions to problems and questions, if they are given any credence at all, are among the least and last considered. With the growth of the behavioral sciences during the past hundred years or so, we have witnessed repeated efforts to identify causes and label solutions that are independent of Jesus Christ and the discipleship to which he has called us.

It is noteworthy that as the number of psychological and sociological explanations provided for misconduct enlarges, as the complexity of the explanation for the problem increases, the spiritual indices and roots of the behavior begin to be disregarded or to be ignored entirely. Thus people—unfortunately including too many members of the Church—spend endless hours seeking to "work through" deep problems rather than repenting of deep sins. Counseling certainly has its place, and a third party (counselor or therapist) whose moral values are intact can do much to help individuals or families recognize and face up to counterproductive attitudes or behaviors. On the other hand, a counselor who operates from a distorted perspective—no matter what the degree of his or her sincerity—cannot lead others to the lasting resolution of their problems. In addition, overmuch counseling can, as Elder Boyd K. Packer warned some years ago, cause the very things we are trying to prevent.[2]

People in our day are reminded continually of what a tense and stress-filled world we live in. The complexity of life and the competition to not only stay afloat but also get ahead have resulted in a host of psychophysiological disorders, maladies that would have been unknown to our forebears. In our naiveté, in our eagerness to handle life in a busy and burdensome world, we are attracted to and occasionally seduced by programs which help us to make it through the night, to get along for now. It is as if Jesus' comforting words had been adapted for a modern age: "Come unto me, all ye that labor and are heavy laden, and I will help you cope." But the Saints really are in a position to do more than cope. Coping implies enduring the present crisis, surviving the moment. Jesus Christ promises deliverance, liberation, lasting peace, not passing pleasure. His solution is not simply to generate and build upon the power of positive thinking. He does not ask us to play Pollyanna, to live in a world of denial. What he does ask of us is that we do all we can to help ourselves and then be willing to shift our remaining burdens to him; what he does require is trust and reliance.

Many preoccupy themselves needlessly with self-inspections; they are compulsively taking their own emotional or spiritual temperatures to assure that they are happy or stable or "together" or worthy. Others spend a lifetime (and too often a fortune) seeking to "find themselves." Again, one of the solemn ironies of existence is the principle found in the words of the Master: "Whosoever will save his life in this world, shall lose it in the world to come. And whosoever will lose his life in this world, for my sake, shall find it in the world to come." (JST, Matthew 16:27-28.)

A more significant undertaking than discovering ourselves is coming to know the Lord. Indeed, as Joseph Smith taught, "If men do not comprehend the character of God, they do not comprehend themselves."[3] The challenge is to seek the Lord, seek to be changed in him, and thereby forget self. "The terrible thing," C. S. Lewis explained, "the almost impossible thing, is to hand over your whole self—all your wishes and precautions—to Christ." He continued:

> But it is far easier than what we are all trying to do instead. For what we are trying to do is to remain what we call "ourselves," to keep personal happiness as our great aim in life, and yet at the same time be "good." We are all trying to let our mind and heart go their own way—centered on money or pleasure or ambition—and hoping, in spite of this, to behave honestly and chastely and humbly. And that is exactly what Christ warned us you could not do. As He said, a thistle cannot produce figs. If I am a field that contains nothing but grass-seed, I cannot produce wheat. Cutting the grass may keep it short: but I shall still produce grass and no wheat. If I want to produce wheat,

the change must go deeper than the surface. I must be ploughed up and re-sown.[4]

In summary, self-discovery or self-esteem are elusive, man-made constructs that must never become an end in themselves. We can feel and become all that we were intended to feel and be, but it will come about in the Lord's own way, through laboring in his cause, serving others, and seeking through him to be remade. "Until you have given up your self to Him you will not have a real self. . . . The very first step [in giving up one's self] is to try to forget about the self altogether. Your real, new self (which is Christ's and also yours, and yours just because it is His) will not come as long as you are looking for it. It will come when you are looking for Him."[5]

Barriers to Grace

There are a number of cultural attitudes and perspectives on life to which we are subject in our modern world. There are trends and movements that militate against an openness and an acceptance of the mercies and grace of Christ. Five of these are discussed below.

1. *Self-Reliance.* Latter-day Saints have been taught (especially in regard to welfare services) that every mature, able-bodied person is responsible for his own care, and that to the extent that this becomes impossible at any point he should explore and exhaust every personal and family resource before turning to the Church or other external sources of assistance. Nor should he shift the burden of care for his own kin beyond the immediate or extended family until all available resources have been expended. And yet one of the harsh realities is that virtues, no matter what the extent of their goodness, can be overdone and thereby become vices. It is so in regard to self-reliance. When a person reaches the point at which he is so autonomous that he is neither God-reliant nor God-dependent, he has constructed a barrier to that enabling power we call the grace of God; he will feel little compulsion to turn to Christ for divine aid. It seems, interestingly enough, that those who cry loudest, "I can handle it!" are so often those who are not handling things very well.

Let me illustrate by recounting two personal experiences that teach the lesson by contrast. I have a friend, an eighty-year-old man, who has smoked since he was a young boy. He is not a member of the

Church, but basically has been and is a very moral and upright person, a respected citizen and a hard worker. I remember asking him years ago, when I was a young boy, "Why don't you stop smoking?" He would respond with something like: "I will one day. I'm working at it." I recall asking him more than once: "Why don't you ask Heavenly Father to help you stop smoking? He would help you if you would ask him." I must have posed that query a dozen times over the years we worked and played together.

To this day I can still remember some of his answers: "Well, son, God helps those who help themselves"; or "Man's extremity is God's opportunity"; or "A man must be willing to give it his all first"; or "A person's gotta pull himself up by his own bootstraps." Lovely statements, aren't they? Sound, practical approaches to life. Kind of a frontier wisdom, I suppose. Very American. I look back on those times now with some degree of humor, but also with some degree of sadness. My friend never did stop smoking. He has emphysema now and struggles and coughs with every breath as he puffs on his cigarette.

Now for the contrasting story. While I was serving as a missionary in the Eastern States during the late 1960s, my companion and I visited a family that had been referred to us by a member of the local ward there in Massachusetts. The first discussion (apostasy and restoration) was well received, and the Spirit of the Lord touched the family's hearts. The second discussion (the Book of Mormon) was likewise accompanied by an unusual spirit, and the family committed themselves to read, ponder, and pray over the book.

When we presented the third lesson (the Word of Wisdom) we encountered a bit of a problem. I asked the father, "Brother Taylor, will you live the Word of Wisdom?" He responded: "Are you asking if I will quit smoking?" We nodded timidly. He continued: "I have smoked two packs of cigarettes a day since I was ten years old. I don't know how I could stop. Is this really necessary before we can join the Church?"

Our hearts sank. These were marvelous people, and the thought of losing them made us sick at heart. I answered even more timidly: "Yes, Brother Taylor, you must live the Word of Wisdom to be baptized. But you can do it. I know you can." He appeared to be touched by my "naive" view of things and asked where he would suddenly receive the desire and the strength to quit.

I blurted out an answer before I thought it through: "If you will simply pray for help, the Lord will give you the strength you need to overcome this habit." I then assured him that if he would drop to his knees every time the urge came, God would take away the urge. He asked: "Do you really believe that?" "I certainly do," I said, with all the maturity and confidence and experience of a nineteen-year-old who had never touched a cigarette in his life!

As we left, my senior companion scolded me. "Why did you say such a thing?" he asked. "What are we going to do when Brother Taylor tries your foolproof plan and fails?" I gulped and apologized.

We returned in a week, nervous and anxious and ready for rejection. My companion had given me the assignment to do the follow-up (since I had been responsible for "botching" the matter in the first place). After greetings and prayer, I asked: "Well, how are you folks doing on the Word of Wisdom?"

Sister Taylor answered: "We finished it."

I didn't understand.

"We finished the pamphlet," she added, referring to the tract we had left.

"Oh," I said. "No, I mean how are you doing in regard to living the Word of Wisdom? Have you been able to stop smoking?"

"Well, yes," Brother Taylor answered in surprised fashion. "You told us the Lord would help us, didn't you? You said we needed to change to be baptized?"

I nodded, dumbfoundedly.

"I did okay for the first seven or eight hours," he said, "and then I had this unbelievable craving to smoke."

"What did you do?" my companion followed up.

"I prayed and asked the Lord to take away the desire to smoke, just like you said to do." He then described a remarkable series of events during the week when simple and direct prayer had resulted in a change of desire. "You guys are right," he remarked. "The Lord really can work miracles if we let him."

There was much weeping and great gratitude expressed to God. We left their home that night sobered and sweetened. The Spirit of the Lord had taken away the veil of unbelief, and the candidate for the kingdom had been born again to see the kingdom of God. A child of God had trusted in a childlike manner in the Lord and in the words of his servants. The family was baptized soon thereafter and sealed as a family unit in holy places a year later.

I am not naive enough to believe that every case is the same or that God will work his marvelous wonders as dramatically in each situation as he did in New England with this little family. Furthermore, as I look back on that experience, I wonder if I could or would be willing to do such a thing today—knowing what I know, being older and more experienced, having a more mature grasp on reality, and being much less childlike in my faith and in my willingness to trust absolutely in the transforming powers of Jehovah. I wonder.

2. *Individualism.* Since the 1960s the American people have been served up a diet of "do your own thing" to the point at which a person may actually feel less than secure, and certainly not in control, if he should submit or give in to the wishes of "the establishment." Elder Neal A. Maxwell has written:

> In today's society, at the mere mention of the words obedience and submissiveness hackles rise and people are put on nervous alert. These virtues are unfashionable because many quickly assume them to be a threat to one's independence and agency. People promptly furnish examples from secular history to illustrate how obedience to unwise authority and servility to bad leaders have caused much human misery and suffering. It is difficult, therefore, to get a hearing for what the words obedience and submissiveness really mean—even when the clarifying phrase, "to God," is attached. We are well conditioned indeed.[6]

People who are possessive of their free will, hesitant to yield and surrender themselves unconditionally to God, will never know the sublime peace and power that come to the true disciple of Jesus Christ. Refusal to submit to divine authority and failure to seek out and follow the Lord's will because of a rabid individualism, will not lead to greater freedom, as supposed, but will instead result in conformity and slavery to the trends, styles, and ideologies of the day. On the other hand, as Elder Boyd K. Packer has instructed, "Obedience to God can be the very highest expression of independence."

> Just think of giving to him the one thing, the one gift, that he would never take. Think of giving him that one thing that he would never wrest from you. . . . Obedience—that which God will never take

by force—he will accept when freely given. And he will then return to you freedom that you can hardly dream of—the freedom to feel and to know, the freedom to do, and the freedom to be, at least a thousand-fold more than we offer him. Strangely enough, the key to freedom is obedience.[7]

3. *Activism and Excellence.* A cartoon picturing a modern-day group of Pharisees in serious reflection upon life has one of the characters stating boldly: "We get our righteousness the old-fashioned way—we earn it!"[8]

We live in a time when the distant voices of the Enlightenment echo the limitless possibilities of man. Seldom does a day go by in which we do not hear the phrase, "In this life you can do anything you set your mind to if you simply work hard enough at it!" Indeed, we ought to do our best. We should stretch ourselves to the limits. In the words of Mormon, "We have a labor to perform whilst in this tabernacle of clay, that we may conquer the enemy of all righteousness, and rest our souls in the kingdom of God" (Moroni 9:6). In the language of King Benjamin, we "should be diligent" (Mosiah 4:27). But there are some things that cannot be worked out by ourselves, some things that are orchestrated and accomplished only in the Lord's way and by his own power. Crucial as it is for us to do "all we can do" (2 Nephi 25:23), we do not conquer the enemy of our souls alone and we do not rest our souls in the celestial kingdom through our own unaided efforts.

One of the fads by which too many Christians have been ensnared is what might be termed the "gospel of success," the tragic and all-too-frequent teaching that righteousness can and will be rewarded by or equated with financial means or worldly recognition. In this regard, one televangelist retold the story of the Rich Young Ruler (Matthew 19:16-22), giving it a rather unusual conclusion. We remember that at the Savior's invitation to sell all that he had and then come and follow Christ, "he went away sorrowful: for he had great possessions." "The televangelist accurately called him a millionaire, and then commented, 'The poor fool! He didn't realize it, but if he had only obeyed Jesus and sacrificed his possessions, Jesus would have made him a billionaire!'"[9] Elder Packer said it best when he observed: "You need not be either rich or hold high position to be completely successful and truly happy. In fact, if these things come to you, and they may, true success must be achieved in spite of them, not because of them. . . . The choice of life is not between fame and obscurity, nor is the choice between wealth and poverty. The choice is between good and evil, and that is a very different matter indeed."[10]

In the last two decades we seem to have developed in the United States a preoccupation with "excellence." Books and tapes and seminars on this abound. Counsel and advice and direction and charts and schemes and planners fill the land. To the degree that such things help us focus on the tasks ahead or to be more effective in what needs to be done, they are commendable. To the degree, however, that our quest for success, our yearning for excellence, leads us to become fiercely competitive, or our desire for improvement results in a fixation upon externals, we are walking in slippery paths. Bruce Hafen has written:

> I am addressing primarily a need for perspective. I do not mean to diminish the value of serious commitments to personal achievement and responsibility. The willingness to strive and keep striving is at the heart of [the scriptural] message to us. But the striving must be to find out God and to accept fully the experiences he knows will enlarge our souls. The trouble with modern pursuits of excellence is that they can become a striving to please other people, or at least to impress them or to seek their approval. A desire for such approval is not all bad, especially among Church members, who generally reserve their approval for accomplishments having positive value. But other people are not finally our judge, and making too much of either the affirmative or the adverse judgments of others can actually undermine our relationship with God and our development of sound values.[11]

It is just so with regard to an inordinate stress upon goal setting and achievement. We should and must have goals in life, and certainly we should do what is appropriate and right to bring them to pass. But our personal goals need to be in harmony with the Lord's grand design for us and for all his children. Further, a too great or unhealthy emphasis in this area can become an obsession with the attainment of goals. If we are not careful this can cause us to be insensitive to people (who may need our assistance but who do not immediately contribute to goal fulfillment) or to those sudden, unexpected promptings of the Spirit (that just might be designed to lead us in unanticipated directions).

4. *Legalism.* In a thirteen-volume work published between 1953 and 1968, Professor Erwin R. Goodenough of Yale University undertook a study of a significant period in Judaism. He described a time wherein what he called "Horizontal Judaism" supplanted and replaced "Vertical Judaism." That is to say, the idea from the beginning that man may engage the Eternal, may commune with his Maker and enjoy fellowship with the heavens (vertical), gave way to the concept that relationship with God is defined solely in terms of one's personal piety, specifically of one's relationship to the Law (horizontal).

In describing the latter, the horizontal—a worldview in Judaism that has survived and is the basis for what we know now as Rabbinic or Pharisaic Judaism—Goodenough wrote: "Man walked through this life along the road God had put before him, a road which was itself the light and law of God, and God above rewarded him for doing so. Man was concerned with proper observances to show respect to God, and with proper attitudes and acts toward his fellow men, but apart from honoring God, he looked to God only for the divine rod and staff to guide him when he was weak." Goodenough explained that "the tension between the two basic types of religious experience . . . , the religion of the vertical path by which man climbs to God and even to a share in divine nature, as over against the legal religion where man walks a horizontal path through this world according to God's instructions," was resolved when Pharisaism won out and the vertical path to God was suppressed and largely forgotten within Judaism. Goodenough then identified similar strains of horizontalism in Christianity, a tendency toward greater institutionalization as growth and acceptance increased.[12]

We Latter-day Saints certainly are not immune from such things. They make their way into the true Church when members become overly concerned with organizational charts at the expense of people, when we place greater stress upon system than sainthood, when we highlight works and downplay grace. Not infrequently, for example, I encounter members who are discouraged, who say in moments of near despair, "I just can't do it all!" Some Latter-day Saints, blocked in their progress by a particular sin and thereby weighed down with guilt, seek to double their effort—to work harder. If the present pace does not eradicate the problem, they decide to run faster. Too often what follows is a type of spiritual diminishing returns—exhaustion and additional frustration. The answer to all problems is not necessarily more and harder work, particularly in regard to spiritual matters. The answer is often to learn our limits and do what we can, then turn to the Lord for assistance.

The Church of Jesus Christ of Latter-day Saints is a divine organization. It administers the gospel. The fulness of salvation will come through the covenants and ordinances made available through the restored Church or it will not come. At the same time, we must never allow our religion to become ritual alone. We must never permit the rules and standards and observances to become so excessive that they become truly burdensome. As the prophets and Apostles have repeatedly beckoned, we must avoid wandering from the ordinances and covenants, from the mission of the Church, from the gifts of the Spirit and the singular spiritual privileges that membership bestows. Both the ancient and the modern oracles hold out to us the most soul-satisfying and sanctifying enterprise in existence, the one venture and undertaking that should consume us and in which we certainly should strive for excellence—the invitation to come unto Christ.

5. *Reducing Sin to Manageable Categories.* A popular approach to repentance involves listing and cataloging one's vices and then allocating sufficient time to conquer each of them. This is a method Benjamin Franklin used. It certainly has merit, and to the degree that people are able to improve by self-effort, the gesture is a commendable one. But it is a terrestrial approach to repentance, and in this sense is inferior to the Lord's system for change. Jesus opens the door for us to become new creatures, totally transformed and totally renewed as to our view of life. In time, through the Atonement and through the sanctifying powers of the Holy Ghost, we can come to abhor sin and, like the people of King Benjamin, "have no more disposition to do evil, but to do good continually" (Mosiah 5:2; compare Alma 13:12).

The issue here may not be obvious. Jesus Christ seeks to help us not just to do good but to *be good.* This entails more than self-discipline, more than pushing ourselves to perfection, gritting our teeth and holding on with white knuckles. And the consequence, the effects upon others, is far more profound than that which follows from a life dedicated to dedication. In the words of C. S. Lewis, the New Testament "talks about Christians 'being born again'; it talks about them 'putting on Christ'; about Christ 'being formed in us';

about our coming to 'have the mind of Christ.'" Lewis then observes that our perception of ourselves—who and what we are as well as what we do—begins to change.

> We begin to notice, besides our particular sinful acts, our sinfulness; begin to be alarmed not only about what we do, but about what we are. This may sound rather difficult, so I will try to make it clear from my own case. When I come to my evening prayers and try to reckon up the sins of the day, nine times out of ten the most obvious one is some sin against charity; I have sulked or snapped or sneered or snubbed or stormed. And the excuse that immediately springs to my mind is that the provocation was so sudden and unexpected: I was caught off my guard, I had not time to collect myself. Now that may be an extenuating circumstance as regards those particular acts: they would obviously be worse if they had been deliberate and premeditated. On the other hand, surely what a man does when he is taken off his guard is the best evidence for what sort of a man he is? Surely what pops out before the man has time to put on a disguise is the truth? If there are rats in a cellar you are most likely to see them if you go in very suddenly. But the suddenness does not create the rats: it only prevents them from hiding. In the same way the suddenness of the provocation does not make me an ill-tempered man: it only shows me what an ill-tempered man I am. . . . And if (as I said before) what we are matters even more than what we do—if, indeed, what we do matters chiefly as evidence of what we are—then it follows that the change which I most need to undergo is a change that my own direct, voluntary efforts cannot bring about. . . . I cannot, by direct moral effort, give myself new motives. After the first few steps in the Christian life we realise that everything which really needs to be done in our souls can be done only by God.[13]

Another writer has described such differences as follows:

> Let me clarify what I mean—the point is important. One friend comes to mind who is self-disciplined in his health habits. He resists temptation to eat too many sweets, he jogs faithfully, and he paces his workload well. I respect him for that. His behavior reflects a commendable level of willpower, a level that sometimes puts to shame my efforts to eat, exercise, and work properly.
>
> Another friend responds to a terribly disappointing and painful struggle in his life by loving others more deeply. He feels his pain but somehow uses it to make himself more aware of others' pain and of

God's ability to encourage. When I look at his life, words like noble, godly, and rich come to mind.

Observing habits of self-discipline, orderliness, and general cordiality do not bring to mind those same words. I describe my well-disciplined friend as effective, respectable, and nice. When I look at his life I think, "I should be more disciplined," I feel a bit pressured, somewhat guilty, and occasionally motivated. The effect of my struggling friend, on the other hand, is not to make me say, "I should be more disciplined," but "I want to be more loving."

The difference is enormous. Some people push me to do better by trying harder. Others draw me to be better by enticing me with an indefinable quality about their lives that seems to grow out of an unusual relationship with Christ, one that really means something, one that goes beyond correct doctrine and appropriate dedication to personally felt reality. . . .

I want to do more than exercise kindness toward my wife; I want to freely give to her from deep resources within me. I want to do more than teach my kids what's expected and then enforce rules to keep them in line; I want to draw them by my life into the pursuit of God. I want to do more than preach sermons that are [scripturally] sound, well delivered, and warmly received; I want to pour out my soul in ways that convey truth with personal power. I want to do more than control my tendency toward depression; I want to taste the goodness of God.[14]

In short, the Lord seeks to transform our nature, not just to modify our behavior. The gospel of Jesus Christ is the power by which we learn to root out the causes of our spiritual illness rather than devoting all our time and exhausting our strength in the alleviation of symptoms.

Conclusion

When the vision of the earth's history is shown, surely we will come to appreciate the heights and depths of the Apostasy, the degree to which people of the earth have unwittingly inherited "lies, vanity, and things wherein there is no profit," the extent to which they have made gods unto themselves which "are no gods" (Jeremiah 16:19-20). Perhaps the saddest part of building broken cisterns that hold precious little of the living water—devising man-made schemes to promote happiness—is the futility of such endeavors; they simply do not produce, cannot deliver the promised rewards. People spend their lives climbing ladders, only at the end of their days to discover that the ladders have been leaning against the wrong wall!

The power of God unto salvation is to be found in and through Jesus Christ and by means of the programs and channels he has appointed. In our day, when speaking of the economic order of heaven, the Savior declared: "It is my purpose to provide for my saints, for all things are mine. But it must needs be done in mine own way." (D&C 104:15-16.) Deliverance from sin and pain is to be found in Christ. On him we must rely. In him only can we rest.

Notes

1. "The False Gods We Worship," *Ensign,* June 1976, p. 4.

2. In Conference Report, April 1978, pp. 135-40.

3. *Teachings of the Prophet Joseph Smith,* sel. Joseph Fielding Smith (Salt Lake City: Deseret Book Co., 1976), p. 343.

4. *Mere Christianity* (New York: Macmillan Publishing Company, 1960), p. 168.

5. C. S. Lewis, *Mere Christianity,* p. 190.

6. *"Not My Will, But Thine"* (Salt Lake City: Bookcraft, 1988), p. 1.

7. "Obedience," *BYU Speeches of the Year* (Provo: BYU Publications, 1972), 7 December 1971, pp. 1-4, 7.

8. Cited in David A. Seamands, *Healing Grace* (Wheaton, Illinois: Victor Books, 1988), p. 34.

9. *Healing Grace,* p. 36.

10. In Conference Report, October 1980, pp. 28-29.

11. *The Broken Heart* (Salt Lake City: Deseret Book Co., 1989), pp. 98-99.

12. See *Jewish Symbols in the Graeco-Roman Period,* ed. and abr. by Jacob Neusner (New Haven: Yale, 1988), pp. 3-35.

13. *Mere Christianity,* pp. 163-65.

14. Larry Crabb, *Inside Out* (Colorado Springs, Colorado: NavPress, 1988), pp. 41-42, italics in original.

Build upon my rock,
which is my gospel.
—D&C 11:24

4

The Best-Kept Secret

*O*ne of the challenges we face in receiving and digesting the myriad truths that have been delivered to the restored Church is to focus on fundamentals, to accentuate the essential. We have so much. We are able to discourse and ponder upon doctrinal matters that are completely mysterious to those outside the faith, matters that must sound like the gibberish of alien tongues to those who have not received the gift of the Holy Ghost. The nature of God, the premortal life, existence in the postmortal spirit world in both paradise and hell, the new and everlasting covenant of marriage, and life in the kingdoms of glory—these are but illustrative of the unspeakable knowledge and intelligence that have been poured out upon the heads of the Lord's people in this final gospel dispensation. These glorious truths are uniquely LDS; they are a part of our heritage and constitute the doctrinal reservoir that helps to make of the Latter-day Saints "a peculiar people" (1 Peter 2:9). And yet Professor Chauncey Riddle at Brigham Young University remarked with good reason some years ago that often the best-kept secret in the Church is the gospel!

The Fundamental Doctrine

There are some truths that are basic and fundamental to our faith, verities that form the foundation for other doctrines. These truths pertain to Jesus Christ and him crucified, and they extend life and light to all other ideas or concepts that we teach and believe. Joseph Smith the Prophet was once asked about the basic tenets of Mormonism. "The fundamental principles of our religion," he answered, "are the testimony of the Apostles and Prophets, concerning Jesus Christ, that He died, was buried, and rose again the third day, and ascended into heaven; and all other things which pertain to our religion are only appendages to it."[1] This statement by the Prophet highlights our duty as to what we ought to teach and what ought to receive the greatest stress in the Church. It suggests that occasionally it may be helpful, relative to our Church involvement, to ask the question, Why are we doing what we are doing? If in fact our efforts do not (directly, or at least indirectly) assist the Saints in their quest to come unto Christ, then perhaps the particular program or activity has no place in the Church.

Latter-day Saints are fond of quoting the passage from the Doctrine and Covenants, "the worth of souls is great in the sight of God." Most often we then skip a few verses and focus upon the joy to be gained from bringing souls into the kingdom through missionary work. But *why* is the worth of souls great in the sight of God? Note the answer in the next verse: "For, behold, the Lord your Redeemer suffered death in the flesh; wherefore, he suffered the pain of all men, that all men might repent and come unto him. And he hath risen again from the dead, that he might bring all men unto him, on conditions of repentance. And how great is his joy in the soul that repenteth!" (D&C 18:10-13.) In short, the worth of souls is great because these souls have been bought with a great price—the price of redemption. People are of infinite worth because their souls have been purchased by one who is infinite and eternal.

And so it is with the Church itself, as well as with all its programs. The Church of Jesus Christ of Latter-day Saints is, in the language of the revelations, "the only true and living church upon the face of the whole earth" (D&C 1:30). The true Church administers the gospel; salvation in this day and age will come through the covenants and ordinances administered and made available by the Church or it will come not at all. It is, however, the gospel that saves (Romans 1:16) and not the Church per se. Auxiliaries and programs and policies and procedures—though essential for the everyday operation and continuing expansion of the Lord's kingdom—are of efficacy, virtue, and force only to the degree that they encourage and motivate the Saints to trust in and serve the Lord and thus receive his matchless mercy and grace.

The word *gospel* means, literally, God-news or good news. The gospel is the good news that Christ came, that he lived and died, and that he rose again to immortal glory. The gospel is the good news that through Christ we may be cleansed and renewed, transformed into new creatures. The gospel is the good news that through our Savior and Redeemer we can be delivered from death and sin to the abundant life. The gospel is thus called "the doctrine of Christ" (2 Nephi 31:2, 21; 32:6; Jacob 7:6). In short, from God's perspective the gospel is "the glad tidings, . . . that he came into the world, even Jesus, to be crucified for the world, and to bear the sins of the world, and to sanctify the world, and to cleanse it from all unrighteousness; that through him all might be saved whom the Father had put into his power and made by him" (D&C 76:40-42). To the Nephites the risen Lord declared: "Behold I have given unto you my gospel, and this is the gospel which I have given unto you—that I came into the world to do the will of my Father, because my Father sent me. And my Father sent me that I might be lifted up upon the cross; and after that I had been lifted up upon the cross, that I might draw all men unto me." (3 Nephi 27:13-14.)

The Principles of the Gospel

From where we stand, the gospel is that divinely given plan and program by which we are able to take advantage of the redemptive labors of the Christ. "Viewed from our mortal position," Elder Bruce R. McConkie wrote, "the gospel is all that is required to take us back to the Eternal Presence, there to be crowned with glory and honor, immortality and eternal life." He continued:

> To gain these greatest of all rewards, two things are required. The first is the atonement by which all men are raised in immortality, with those who believe and obey ascending also unto eternal life. This atoning sacrifice was the work of our Blessed Lord, and he has done his work. The second requisite is obedience on our part to the laws and ordinances of the gospel. Thus the gospel is, in effect, the atonement. But the gospel is also all of the laws, principles, doctrines, rites, ordinances, acts, powers, authorities, and keys needed to save and exalt fallen man in the highest heaven hereafter.[2]

In a revelation given to the Church in our day, the Lord commanded: "Open your mouths and they shall be filled, saying: Repent, repent, and prepare ye the way of the Lord, and make his paths straight; for the kingdom of heaven is at hand; yea, repent and be baptized, every one of you, for a remission of your sins; yea, be baptized even by water, and then cometh the baptism of fire and of the Holy Ghost. Behold, verily, verily, I say unto you, this is my gospel." (D&C 33:10-12.) To James Covill, the Savior explained:

> Hearken and listen to the voice of him who is from all eternity to all eternity, the Great I Am, even Jesus Christ—
>
> The light and the life of the world; a light which shineth in darkness and the darkness comprehendeth it not;
>
> The same which came in the meridian of time unto mine own, and mine own received me not;
>
> But to as many as received me, gave I power to become my sons; and even so will I give unto as many as will receive me, power to become my sons.
>
> And verily, verily, I say unto you, he that receiveth my gospel receiveth me; and he that receiveth not my gospel receiveth not me.
>
> And this is my gospel—repentance and baptism by water, and then cometh the baptism of fire and the Holy Ghost, even the Comforter, which showeth all things, and teacheth the peaceable things of the kingdom. (D&C 39:1-6.)

The scriptures clearly and consistently teach that the principles of the gospel are as follows:

1. *Faith in the Lord Jesus Christ.* Those who desire to enjoy the benefits of the atonement of Christ must learn to exercise faith in Christ. They must believe in him, believe that he is, "that he created all things, both in heaven and in earth; believe that he has all wisdom, and all power, both in heaven and in earth; believe that man doth not comprehend all the things which the Lord can comprehend" (Mosiah 4:9). In the *Lectures on Faith* Joseph Smith taught that three things are necessary in order for any rational and intelligent being to exercise saving faith in God or Christ. First, a person must accept the idea that God actually exists; he must plant the seed of faith in his heart and experiment upon (pray over and labor with) the fact that there actually is a Savior and Messiah (see Alma 32-33). Second, the person must have a correct idea of God's character, attributes, and perfec-

tions; he must from serious study and personal revelation seek to understand what God is like. Third, he must gain an actual knowledge that the course of life he is pursuing accords with the will of God; he must know that his life is worthy of divine approbation and thus of the blessings of heaven. The Prophet explained that the latter requisite for faith—the peaceful assurance that one has pleased God—comes only through one's willingness to sacrifice all things for the kingdom's sake. Faith in Jesus Christ, the first principle of the gospel, is thus based upon evidence. And the more evidence one amasses—external and internal—the greater one's faith. We may begin with the simple hope that there is a Christ and that salvation is available (see Alma 32:27), but in time that hope can, by the power of the Holy Ghost, ripen into the knowledge that one day we will not only be with Christ but also be like him (see 1 John 3:2; Moroni 7:41, 48).

2. *Repentance.* Once a person comes to know the Lord—of his power and greatness and perfections—he automatically senses his own inadequacies. He feels to shrink before the Lord Omnipotent; he cries out for mercy and pardon from the Holy One of Israel. And thus it is that repentance follows on the heels of faith: as we encounter the Master, we begin to discern the vast chasm between the divine realm and our own unholy state. Repentance is literally an "afterthought," a "change of mind," a change in perspective and a change in life-style. Repentance is the process by which we discard the rags of uncleanness and through Christ begin to adorn ourselves with the robes of righteousness. It is the means by which we incorporate into our lives a power beyond our own, an infinite power that transforms us into new creatures, new creatures in Christ.

3. *Baptism, by water and by fire.* Jesus and his prophets have declared in unmistakable terms that salvation comes only to those who have been born again (see John 3:1-5; Mosiah 27:24-26; Alma 7:14). People must be born again in order to see and enter the kingdom of God. When the Spirit of the Lord takes the veil of darkness and unbelief from their eyes they are born again to *see*, and they are thereby enabled to recognize and acknowledge the Lord's church and his servants. They are born again to *enter* the kingdom only as they receive the appropriate ordinances of salvation and continue faithful thereafter. Baptism becomes the physical token of our acceptance of the atoning graces of Christ. We go down into the "watery

grave" and come forth as initiates, new citizens of the kingdom, even as a sign of our ready acceptance of the Lord's burial in the tomb and his subsequent rise to newness of life in the Resurrection (see Romans 6:3-5). The baptism of fire takes place as the Holy Ghost, who is a sanctifier, takes from our souls the filth and dross of worldliness. "Lay aside every sin," Alma pleaded with the people of Gideon, "which easily doth beset you, which doth bind you down to destruction, yea, come and go forth, and show unto your God that ye are willing to repent of your sins and enter into a covenant with him to keep his commandments, and witness it unto him this day by going into the waters of baptism" (Alma 7:15). The Prophet Joseph Smith taught that "baptism is a sign to God, to angels, and to heaven that we do the will of God, and there is no other way beneath the heavens whereby God hath ordained for man to come to Him to be saved, and enter into the Kingdom of God, except faith in Jesus Christ, repentance, and baptism for the remission of sins, and any other course is in vain; then you have the promise of the gift of the Holy Ghost."[3] Those who are born again become sons and daughters of Christ and heirs to the heavenly kingdom (see D&C 25:1; 34:3).

4. *Enduring to the end.* Disciples of Christ in all ages are instructed to be baptized of water and of fire, and then to labor to maintain their worthy standing before God. To endure to the end is to keep the commandments after baptism, to strive to live the life of a Saint thereafter. The commission is for members of the household of faith to "stand as witnesses of God at all times and in all things, and in all places that ye may be in, even until death, that ye may be redeemed of God, and be numbered with those of the first resurrection, that ye may have eternal life" (Mosiah 18:9). To endure to the end is to be "steadfast and immovable"—the scriptural phrase for spiritual maturity—"always abounding in good works, that Christ, the Lord God Omnipotent, may seal you his, that you may be brought to heaven, that ye may have everlasting salvation and eternal life" (Mosiah 5:15). Nephi explained that "unless a man shall endure to the end, in following the example of the Son of the living God, he cannot be saved." Further, "ye must press forward with a steadfastness in Christ, having a perfect brightness of hope, and a love of God and of all men. Wherefore, if ye shall press forward, feasting upon the word of Christ, and endure to the end, behold, thus saith the Father:

Ye shall have eternal life." (2 Nephi 31:16, 20; compare 33:4; 3 Nephi 27:16; D&C 6:13; 14:7.)

5. *Resurrection and eternal judgment.* Joseph Smith explained in 1839 that "the doctrines of the Resurrection of the Dead and the Eternal Judgment are necessary to preach among the first principles of the Gospel of Jesus Christ."[4] Through the atonement of Jesus Christ, as an unconditional benefit, all men and women will, in a certain sense, be redeemed from spiritual death. They will be raised from the grave and thereafter brought to stand in the presence of the Almighty to be judged according to the deeds done in the body. This principle of the gospel illustrates both the mercy and the justice of God. "It shall come to pass," Jacob prophesied, "that when all men shall have passed from this first death unto life, insomuch as they have become immortal, they must appear before the judgment-seat of the Holy One of Israel; and then cometh the judgment, and then must they be judged according to the holy judgment of God." Jacob's witness was that the Lord of Life would suffer "the pains of all men, yea, the pains of every living creature, . . . that the resurrection might pass upon all men, that all might stand before him at the great and judgment day." (2 Nephi 9:15, 21-22.) Samuel the Lamanite similarly testified that Christ "surely must die that salvation may come; yea, it behooveth him and becometh expedient that he dieth, to bring to pass the resurrection of the dead, that thereby men may be brought into the presence of the Lord" (Helaman 14:15).

The Book of Mormon is said to contain the fulness of the gospel (see D&C 20:9; 27:5; 42:12). Some have wondered how the Lord and his prophets could state this, when in fact the Book of Mormon contains no reference to such matters as eternal marriage, degrees of glory, work for the dead, and so forth. Again, let us focus upon what the gospel is. The Book of Mormon contains the fulness of the gospel in the sense that it teaches the doctrines of redemption—that salvation is in Christ and in him alone—and the principles of the gospel (faith, repentance, rebirth, enduring, resurrection, and judgment) more plainly and persuasively than any other book of scripture. The Book of Mormon does not necessarily contain the fulness of gospel doctrine. Rather, it is a sacred repository of eternal truth relative to the most fundamental doctrine of all—the doctrine of Christ. In the words of President Ezra Taft Benson: "The Book of Mormon contains the 'fulness of the gospel of Jesus Christ.' (D&C 20:9.) That does not mean it contains every teaching, every doctrine ever revealed. Rather, it means that in the Book of Mormon we will find the fulness of those doctrines required for our salvation. And they are taught plainly and simply so that even children can learn the ways of salvation and exaltation."[5]

What Shall We Teach?

We have received a divine commission from our Lord to teach one another the doctrine of the kingdom (D&C 88:77). What is it that we should teach? Above and beyond all that might be said in sermons and lessons and seminars and discussions, what should be the walk and talk of the Latter-day Saints? Simply stated, we are to teach the gospel. Our primary message, like Paul's, must be "Jesus Christ, and him crucified" (1 Corinthians 2:2). If we have any hope of preserving the faith of our fathers among our people, of building firmly on the rock of revelation and the doctrines Joseph Smith taught, then we must ground and settle ourselves in Jesus Christ and his atoning sacrifice. We must, of course, teach all of the doctrines of the gospel when it is appropriate to do so. But above all we must see to it that "we talk of Christ, we rejoice in Christ, we preach of Christ, we prophesy of Christ, . . . that our children may know to what source they may look for a remission of their sins" (2 Nephi 25:26).

In 1981 Commissioner Henry B. Eyring delivered an address to teachers in the Church Educational System. He spoke soberly of the "sea of filth" that the young people of today encounter, and of the absolute necessity for solid and sound gospel instruction in an effort to immunize the youth against the waywardness of the world.

> Now I would like to say this: There are two views of the gospel—both true. They make a terrific difference in the power of your teaching. One view is that the gospel is all truth. It is. The gospel is truth. With that view I could teach pretty well anything true in a classroom, and I would be teaching the gospel. The other view is that the gospel is the principles, commandments, and ordinances which, if kept, conformed with, and accepted, will lead to eternal life. That is also true.
>
> When I choose which of these views I will let dominate my teaching, I take a great step. If I take the view that the gospel is all

truth, rather than that it is the ordinances and principles and commandments which, if kept, conformed with, and accepted, lead to eternal life, I have already nearly taken myself out of the contest to help a student withstand the sea of filth. Why? Because he needs to have his eyes focused on light, and that means not truth in some abstract sense but the joy of keeping the commandments and conforming with the principles and accepting the ordinances of the gospel of Jesus Christ. If I decide I will not make that my primary vision of the gospel, I am already out of the contest to help my student with his capacity to see good and to want and desire it in the midst of filth.[6]

There is power in the gospel, supernal power in the glad tidings of Christ and his ministry of reconciliation. There is power in the principles of the gospel, a transforming power that can and does flow into the lives of those who exercise faith in Christ, repent unto Christ, are born anew unto Christ, and endure faithfully through Christ's assistance. The ancients were bold and unashamed and so must we be. "I am not ashamed of the gospel of Christ," Paul declared, "for it is the power of God unto salvation to every one that believeth" (Romans 1:16).

In a day when teachers in the Church may feel that they are forced to compete with extravagant media or modern technology, we must trust that the preaching of the word—the simple proclamation of the gospel by the power of the Holy Ghost—has "a great tendency to lead the people to do that which [is] just—yea, it [has] had more powerful effect upon the minds of the people than . . . anything else." To accept and apply this principle is to "try the virtue of the word of God." (Alma 31:5.) Further, "When a teacher feels he must blend worldly sophistication and erudition to the simple principles of the gospel or to our Church history so that his message will have more appeal and respectability to the academically learned, he has compromised his message. We seldom impress people by this means and almost never convert them to the gospel."[7]

Conclusion

The gospel is the glad tidings concerning the infinite and eternal atoning sacrifice of Jesus Christ. The Atonement is central. It is the hub of the wheel; all other matters are as spokes. Related doctrines are important, but they are auxiliary to the gospel and thus receive power and life to the degree that they are anchored in and tied to the pure doctrine of Christ. "The atonement of Christ is the most basic and fundamental doctrine of the gospel," Elder Bruce R. McConkie stated in his last address to the Church, "and it is the least understood of all our revealed truths." He went on:

> Many of us have a superficial knowledge and rely upon the Lord and his goodness to see us through the trials and perils of life.
>
> But if we are to have faith like Enoch and Elijah we must believe what they believed, know what they knew, and live as they lived.
>
> May I invite you to join with me in gaining a sound and sure knowledge of the Atonement.
>
> We must cast aside the philosophies of men and the wisdom of the wise and hearken to that Spirit which is given to us to guide us into all truth.
>
> We must search the scriptures, accepting them as the mind and will and voice of the Lord and the very power of God unto salvation.[8]

The gospel must never be a secret to those of the true Church. Rather, it must be studied and taught and declared, as well as felt in the hearts and souls of those who have chosen to come unto Christ. It ought to accent our teachings and influence for good our whole approach to life. Christ's church must be called after his name; it must also be built upon his gospel. "And if it so be that the church is built upon [his] gospel then will the Father show forth his own works in it" (3 Nephi 27:10). In our own dispensation the Lord assured Hyrum Smith that if he sought the kingdom of God "all things shall be added according to that which is just." And then came the timeless command: "Build upon my rock, which is my gospel." (D&C 11:23-24.)

Notes

1. *Teachings of the Prophet Joseph Smith,* sel. Joseph Fielding Smith (Salt Lake City: Deseret Book Co., 1976), p. 121.

2. *A New Witness for the Articles of Faith* (Salt Lake City: Deseret Book Co., 1985), p. 134.

3. *Teachings of the Prophet Joseph Smith,* p. 198.

4. *Teachings of the Prophet Joseph Smith*, p. 149; see also p. 365.

5. *A Witness and a Warning* (Salt Lake City: Deseret Book Co., 1988), pp. 18-19.

6. "Eyes to See, Ears to Hear," in *The Eighth Annual Church Educational System Religious Educators' Symposium, New Testament* (Salt Lake City: The Church of Jesus Christ of Latter-day Saints, 1984), p. 11.

7. Ezra Taft Benson, "The Gospel Teacher and His Message," in *Charge to Religious Educators*, 2nd ed. (Salt Lake City: The Church of Jesus Christ of Latter-day Saints, 1982), p. 48.

8. In Conference Report, April 1985, p. 11.

To some it is given by the Holy Ghost to know
that Jesus Christ is the Son of God,
and that he was crucified for the sins of the world.
—D&C 46:13

5

———

The Revelation of Christ

The angel explained to John on Patmos that "the testimony of Jesus is the spirit of prophecy" (Revelation 19:10). The primary responsibility of a prophet is to stand as a witness of the Lord Jesus— to bear testimony of him and of the salvation that comes in and through his holy name. In the words of Peter, "to [Christ] give all the prophets witness" (Acts 10:43). Jacob observed that "none of the prophets have written, nor prophesied, save they have spoken concerning this Christ" (Jacob 7:11). And what is true of prophets is equally true of members of the Church who have received the gift of the Holy Ghost. Prophets are our pattern; they receive and deliver the witness and thus set the example for all to follow. As Moses concluded, "Would God that all the Lord's people were prophets, and that the Lord would put his spirit upon them!" (Numbers 11:29.)

The Latter-day Revelation of Christ

It was on the morning of a beautiful, clear day in the spring of 1820. The long night of apostate darkness was brought to a close by the appearance of two heavenly beings to a fourteen-year-old boy. The very presence of these glorious resurrected personages attested to the reality of life after death, and their message signaled the times of restitution of all things (see Acts 3:21). In the words of Joseph Smith, "One of them spake unto me, calling me by name and said, pointing to the other—*This is My Beloved Son. Hear Him!*" (Joseph Smith—History 1:17). The First Vision, which might be called the beginning of the revelation of God to man in this dispensation, was likewise the beginning of the revelation of Christ. Through the subsequent revelations given to Joseph Smith and his successors, the knowledge of a Savior and of the principles whereby men and women might come to enjoy a meaningful spiritual union with him has come anew to mankind.

It is worth a moment's reflection to consider the kinds of truths God has mercifully and bountifully made known since that glorious morning in the Sacred Grove. (A number of these doctrines will be developed and documented in more depth in subsequent chapters.) To begin with, Joseph Smith learned that the Father and the Son are separate and distinct personages, that Jesus of Nazareth was not simply one manifestation of a triune God. Through the Book of Mormon and later revelations, the Saints have gained insights into the role of Jesus Christ as Jehovah, the premortal God of the ancients, the Holy One of Israel. By means of latter-day revelation we understand the role of Jehovah as the Creator of worlds without number, ages before he was tabernacled in flesh.

Further, we learn of a significant verity of Christ's eternal gospel—the knowledge that Christian prophets have declared Christian doctrine and administered Christian ordinances since the days of Adam. Enoch had the testimony of Jesus. Noah preached in the name of Christ. Moses worshiped the Father in the name of the Son. These things, once obvious and evident to a religious world, are not so today, largely because of the plain and precious things removed from the biblical records by an organization that was "great and abominable." The prophets have borne repeated testimony of the fact that all revelation since the fall of man has come by and through Jesus Christ, the God of the Old Testament. Whenever the Father has manifested himself, he has done so to introduce and bear witness of the Son.

One of the most helpful and inspirational explanations from the leadership of the Church in this dispensation concerns Christ's ministry as both the Father and the Son. With the added insight, for example, that Jesus can and does speak and act by divine investiture of authority—in behalf of the Father—the scriptures take on a whole new meaning and our knowledge of the unity of Elohim and Jehovah expands greatly.

Perhaps one of the most poignant revelations of the Restoration—a knowledge enjoyed by the Latter-day Saints alone—pertains to the suffering of Jesus in Gethsemane. When through the prophetic word in the Doctrine and Covenants and through latter-day oracles we gain but a glimpse of our Savior's suffering—begun in Gethsemane and consummated on the cross—we are in a position to feel and express gratitude to our Mediator to a degree that otherwise would have been impossible. And who can measure the worth of President Joseph F. Smith's vision of Christ's postmortal ministry among the disembodied? (D&C 138.) Through this majestic manifestation the biblical information on this event is greatly enhanced, and the Saints receive inspiring detail on how our Lord's service to mankind spanned the veil and linked the heavens with the earth.

Finally, let us observe gratefully that it is through latter-day scripture—particularly the Book of Mormon—that the otherwise insurmountable doctrinal difficulties surrounding grace and works are handled with prophetic precision by righteous ancients who knew their God and gloried in his mercies. What more can we say? We thank thee, O God, for prophets!

Come, Know the Lord

The everlasting gospel has been restored to earth in order that men and women may come unto Christ, make sacred covenants with him, rejoice in and receive his saving graces, and in due course acquire his divine nature. In fact, God has set his hand again the second time to gather Israel in order "that every man might speak in the name of God the Lord, even the Savior of the world" (D&C 1:20). This is a Church of full participation. The Lord never intended that the prophets and Apostles be the only persons on earth (and certainly in the true Church) who think or reason or receive revelation. And the God of heaven certainly never ordained that only prophets, seers, and revelators for the Church be the possessors of the witness and knowledge of the Lord.

The Lord has said: "To some it is given by the Holy Ghost to know that Jesus Christ is the Son of God, and that he was crucified for the sins of the world." Such persons have sought and prayed and received that sacred witness that comes to all who ask in faith. These have gained the assurance—by the power of the Holy Ghost and often through a personal application of the Atonement—that Jesus lives, that he lifts and lightens, that he loves. "To others it is given to believe on their words, that they also might have eternal life if they continue faithful." (D&C 46:13-14.) In writing of the latter group, of those who, while seeking to obtain their own witness, trust in the testimony of others, Elder Bruce R. McConkie observed:

> Prophets and apostles and the elders of Israel preach the gospel and testify of Christ and his divine Sonship, having first received the divine message by personal revelation. Some believe their words and know in their hearts that they have heard the truth. The truths taught may be new and strange to the hearers, but their acceptance is instinctive, automatic, without restraint; they need hear no further arguments. The Spirit-guided words find firm lodgment in their souls by the power of the Spirit. This ability to believe is a gift of God.
>
> Individuals who have not yet advanced in spiritual things to the point of gaining for themselves personal and direct revelation from the Holy Ghost may yet have power to believe what others, speaking by the power of the Spirit, both teach and testify. They have power to recognize the truth of the words of others who do speak by the power of the Spirit, even though they cannot attune themselves to the Infinite so as to receive the divine word direct from heaven and without the helps of others to teach them. . . . Thus, men can obey and be saved even though they do not see the Lord, or entertain angels, or receive, independent of any other persons, the heaven-sent word of salvation.[1]

The testimony of Jesus, the knowledge that makes every person who possesses it a prophet,[2] comes by the power of the Holy Ghost. Such a witness, when nourished and cultivated, becomes an indelible source of spiritual confidence and an undeviating guide. "As I pray for the guidance of the Spirit," President Harold B. Lee explained to Brigham Young University students just before his death, "and seek to rise to the responsibility which has been given me, I don't ask for any special endowment. I ask only to go where the Lord would have me go, and only to receive what the Lord would have me receive, knowing that more important than sight is the witness that one may have by the witness of the Holy Ghost to his soul that things are so and that Jesus is the Christ, a living personage. It is that which guides me through many of the experiences of life." And then, in stressing how such a conviction can provide the anchor to life and the standard for one's actions, President Lee said: "You Latter-day Saints, the youth of the noble birthright, if you can say, as Martha said, 'Yea, Lord, I believe that thou art the Christ, the Son of God, which should come into the world' [see John 11:25-27]—if you can say that and know that he is in his heaven, and you believe that with all your soul, you will not be trapped in the pitfalls of life."[3]

It is through the Bible that we are able to learn details concerning the mortal sojourn of the one perfect being. His example is laid before us and his pattern for living stands as a beacon for all humanity. Through modern revelation we come to understand the doctrine of Christ—the gospel, the plan of salvation, the theological foundation of our religion, and the principles that bring us to the author of our faith. More important, however, the scriptures—the institutional revelations—and the words of the prophets teach us how we may, through individual revelation, come through the power of the Spirit to know God and thereby gain the mind of Christ. If it is life eternal to know the only true God and Jesus Christ whom he has sent (John 17:3), then surely the means for coming to know them must be made known. And so it has. That plan, that system of salvation, that means whereby we become reacquainted with the Father and the Son—this we call the gospel of Jesus Christ. It is "the power of God unto salvation" (Romans 1:16).

Conclusion

Speaking to Joseph Smith in 1829, Jesus Christ said: "This generation shall have my word through you" (D&C 5:10). If salvation is to come to people in this dispensation, it will come through the gospel restored through Joseph Smith and the Church which administers that gospel and its attendant ordinances. As a revelator and a restorer, Joseph Smith's preeminent duty was to make known the Gods of heaven and set forth the divine plan that enables fallen men and women to come unto Christ and be perfected in him. Joseph's testimony of the Christ was perfect. "And now," the Prophet and Sidney Rigdon attested, "after the many testimonies which have been given of him [the Savior], this is the testimony, last of all, which we give of him: That he lives! For we saw him, even on the right hand of God; and we heard the voice bearing record that he is the Only Begotten of the Father—that by him, and through him, and of him, the worlds are and were created, and the inhabitants thereof are begotten sons and daughters unto God." (D&C 76:22-24.)

Joseph Smith's knowledge of the divine was absolute. And his witness, which has been or will be carried to all nations, will be perpetuated until the Holy One returns and the knowledge of God covers the earth, as the waters cover the sea.

Notes

1. *A New Witness for the Articles of Faith* (Salt Lake City: Deseret Book Co., 1985), p. 372.

2. See *Teachings of the Prophet Joseph Smith*, sel. Joseph Fielding Smith (Salt Lake City: Deseret Book Co., 1976), pp. 119, 160.

3. "Be Loyal to the Royal Within You," *1973 BYU Speeches of the Year* (Provo: BYU Publications, 1974), pp. 88, 102.

It must needs be that the Gentiles be convinced also
that Jesus is the Christ, the Eternal God.
—2 Nephi 26:12

6

The Condescension of God

*F*rom the time of the First Vision, in 1820, Joseph the Prophet knew that the Father and the Son were separate individuals. Joseph Smith instructed the School of the Prophets: "God is the only supreme governor and independent being in whom all fullness and perfection dwell; who is omnipotent, omnipresent and omniscient; without beginning of days or end of life; and . . . in him every good gift and every good principle dwell; and . . . he is the Father of lights."[1] In April 1843 Joseph the Prophet gave a simple explanation that has profound theological implications: "The Father has a body of flesh and bones as tangible as man's; the Son also; but the Holy Ghost has not a body of flesh and bones, but is a personage of Spirit" (D&C 130:22).

By 1844 the Prophet was able to deliver the crowning pronouncements of his ministry regarding the person and nature of God. In the King Follett Discourse, Joseph Smith taught: "God himself was once as we are now, and is an exalted man, and sits enthroned in yonder heavens! That is the great secret." Continuing: "It is the first principle of the Gospel to know for a certainty the Character of God, and to know that we may converse with him as one man converses with another, and that he was once a man like us; yea, that God himself, the Father of us all, dwelt on an earth, the same as Jesus Christ himself did."[2]

President Joseph Fielding Smith provided the following insight regarding the ministries of Elohim and Jehovah: "After Adam's transgression he was shut out of the presence of the Father who has remained hidden from his children to this day, with few exceptions wherein righteous men have been privileged with the glorious privilege of seeing him. The withdrawal of the Father did not break the communication between men and God, for another means of approach was instituted and that is through the ministry of his Beloved Son, Jesus Christ."[3]

President Smith further explained: "All revelation since the fall has come through Jesus Christ, who is the Jehovah of the Old Testament. In all of the scriptures, where God is mentioned and where he has appeared, it was Jehovah. . . . The Father has never dealt with man directly and personally since the fall, and he has never appeared except to introduce and bear record of the Son."[4]

It is very clear from the scriptures that while Jehovah-Christ is the God who deals directly with man, Elohim, the Eternal Father, is the ultimate object of man's worship. A modern revelation at the time of the organization of the restored Church explained:

> By these things [specifically the teachings of the Book of Mormon and modern revelations] we know that there is a God in heaven, who is infinite and eternal, from everlasting to everlasting the same unchangeable God, the framer of heaven and earth, and all things which are in them;
> And that he created man, male and female, after his own image and in his own likeness, created he them;
> And gave unto them commandments that they should love and serve him, the only living and true God, and that he should be the only being whom they should worship (D&C 20:17-19; compare JST, John 4:25-26).

Lehi spoke of God the Eternal Father as the "Lord God" who would raise up a Messiah among the Jews, even a Savior of the world (1 Nephi 10:4). Nearly fifty years later, Nephi spoke of the scattering and gathering of Israel, and especially the Jews:

> And after they have been scattered, and the Lord God hath scourged them by other nations for the space of many generations, yea, even down from generation to generation until they shall be persuaded to believe in Christ, the Son of God, and the atonement, which is infinite for all mankind—and when that day shall come that they *shall*

believe in Christ, and worship the Father in his name, . . . the Lord will set his hand again the second time to restore his people from their lost and fallen state. Wherefore, he will proceed to do a marvelous work and a wonder among the children of men. (2 Nephi 25:16-17, italics added.)

The Book of Mormon record contains abundant references to the distinct personalities of Elohim, the Father, and Jehovah, or Jesus Christ, the Son (see, for example, 2 Nephi 30:2; 31:7-21; 32:9; 33:12; Jacob 4:5; Alma 5:48; 12:33-34; Moroni 4:3; 5:2; 7:22-27, 32, 48). Generally, however, the Book of Mormon prophets make reference to "God" or "the Lord" without any indication of whether Elohim or Jehovah was intended. Elder Bruce R. McConkie has observed:

> Most scriptures that speak of God or of the Lord do not even bother to distinguish the Father from the Son, simply because it doesn't make any difference which God is involved. They are one. The words or deeds of either of them would be the words and deeds of the other in the same circumstances.
>
> Further, if a revelation comes from, or by the power of the Holy Ghost, ordinarily the words will be those of the Son, though what the Son says will be what the Father would say, and the words may thus be considered as the Father's.[5]

Sometimes in our zeal to declare and establish the distinction between the two personages, we fail to appreciate properly the importance of their oneness. Though they are separate personages, their distinctive unity is the great example and goal, as signified by the words of the risen Lord to the three Nephite disciples: "Ye shall be even as I am, and I am even as the Father; and the Father and I are one" (3 Nephi 28:10; see also 11:27, 36).

The Eternal God

On the title page of the Book of Mormon we learn of the major purposes of that sacred volume. Moroni there explains that the records had been kept and preserved "to show unto the remnant of the House of Israel what great things the Lord hath done for their fathers; and that they may know the covenants of the Lord, that they are not cast off forever—and also to the convincing of the Jew and

Gentile that Jesus is the Christ, the Eternal God, manifesting himself unto all nations."

The Book of Mormon is Another Testament of Jesus Christ: it confirms the historical veracity of Jesus of Nazareth, bears witness of his divine sonship, and serves as an accompanying testament with the Bible. The Book of Mormon helps, of course, to sustain and reinforce the messianic testimonies of the New Testament prophets and Apostles. But it does more than this. Nephi explained, "And as I spake concerning the convincing of the Jews, that Jesus is the very Christ, it must needs be that the Gentiles be convinced also that *Jesus is the Christ, the Eternal God*" (2 Nephi 26:12, italics added).

The Book of Mormon prophets certify that Jesus Christ is the Eternal God. That is, the Book of Mormon is a witness to the fact that Christ is God, the Eternal One, that he was God in the premortal existence before this world was formed, that he is the Jehovah of the Old Testament, the God of the ancient patriarchs, the Holy One of Israel, and that he will forever be God to us. Had we access to all the records of all the prophets who knew God from the beginning, undoubtedly we would see as central to their experiences or their writings the unmistakable witness that Christ was and is the Eternal God. The Book of Mormon has come to us untainted and unhampered, and thus we find within its covers this repeated announcement.

In stressing the importance of Latter-day Saints viewing Christ for who and what he really is, Elder Bruce R. McConkie wrote:

> Christ-Messiah is God!
>
> Such is the plain and pure pronouncement of all the prophets of all the ages. In our desire to avoid the false and absurd conclusions contained in the creeds of Christendom, we are wont to shy away from this pure and unadorned verity; we go to great lengths to use language that shows there is both a Father and a Son, that they are separate Persons and are not somehow mystically intertwined as an essence or spirit that is everywhere present. Such an approach is perhaps essential in reasoning with the Gentiles of sectarianism; it helps to overthrow the fallacies formulated in their creeds.
>
> But having so done, if we are to envision our Lord's true status and glory, we must come back to the pronouncement of pronouncements, the doctrine of doctrines, the message of messages, which is that Christ is God. And if it were not so, he could not save us.[6]

One of the strongest chapters in the Book of Mormon attesting to the role of Christ as the Eternal God is 1 Nephi 11. Nephi's pondering and prayer in response to his father's dream resulted in a remarkable vision (1 Nephi 11-14). As recorded in chapter 11, Nephi's divinely sent guide began with the explanation of the tree that Lehi had seen. Nephi was caught away into a vision: "And it came to pass that I looked and beheld the great city of Jerusalem, and also other cities. And I beheld the city of Nazareth; and in the city of Nazareth I beheld a virgin, and she was exceedingly fair and white." (1 Nephi 11:13.) Nephi was asked by the angel, "Knowest thou the condescension of God?" He answered, "I know that he loveth his children; nevertheless, I do not know the meaning of all things." (1 Nephi 11:16-17.)

Nephi seemed to grasp the fact that the great God has love and compassion for his earthly children, and that he condescends in the sense that he who is infinite and perfect has tender regard for those who are so very finite and imperfect. But the angel had much more in mind. "And he said unto me: Behold, the virgin whom thou seest is the mother of the Son of God, after the manner of the flesh." Nephi witnessed as Mary was "carried away in the Spirit." "And I looked and beheld the virgin again, bearing a child in her arms. And the angel said unto me: Behold the Lamb of God, yea, even the Son of the Eternal Father!" (1 Nephi 11:18-21.) Nephi observed while the Eternal One—Jehovah, who would come to be known as Jesus Christ—went forth among the children of men "ministering unto the people, in power and great glory; and the multitudes were gathered together to hear him; and I beheld that they cast him out from among them" (1 Nephi 11:28). Nephi thereafter bore witness of the irony of the ages—the greatest contradiction of eternity:[7] "And I looked and beheld the Lamb of God, that he was taken by the people; yea, the Son of the everlasting God was judged of the world; and I saw and bear record. And I, Nephi, saw that he was lifted up upon the cross and slain for the sins of the world." (1 Nephi 11:32-33.)

Jacob bore a similar testimony: "I know that ye know that in the body he [Christ] shall show himself unto those at Jerusalem, from whence we came; for it is expedient that it should be among them; for it behooveth the great Creator that he suffereth himself to become subject unto man in the flesh, and die for all men, that all men might become subject unto him" (2 Nephi 9:5). In similar fashion an angel explained to King Benjamin concerning the condescension of God:

> For behold, the time cometh, and is not far distant, that with power, the Lord Omnipotent who reigneth, who was, and is from all eternity to all eternity, shall come down from heaven among the children of men, and shall dwell in a tabernacle of clay. . . .
>
> And lo, he shall suffer temptations, and pain of body, hunger, thirst, and fatigue, even more than man can suffer, except it be unto death; for behold, blood cometh from every pore, so great shall be his anguish for the wickedness and the abominations of his people. . . .
>
> And lo, he cometh unto his own, that salvation might come unto the children of men even through faith on his name; and even after all this they shall consider him a man, and say that he hath a devil, and shall scourge him, and shall crucify him. (Mosiah 3:5, 7, 9; compare 1 Nephi 19:7-10; 2 Nephi 1:10.)

Indeed, nothing is more plain in the Book of Mormon than the fact that the God of ancient Israel, the God of their fathers, would come to earth as the mortal Messiah, would "descend from his throne divine" to rescue rebellious souls and thus make salvation available to the penitent.[8]

The confrontation between Amulek and Zeezrom provides invaluable insights into the role of Jehovah as premortal God and mortal Savior. Zeezrom, crafty and skilled in his rhetorical devices, sought to cross and embarrass Amulek "that he might destroy that which was good." Zeezrom asked, "Thou sayest there is a true and living God?" to which Amulek responded, "Yea, there is a true and living God." Zeezrom followed up: "Is there more than one God?" to which the Nephite missionary answered simply, "No." Amulek had answered correctly on two counts. There is only *one Godhead,* as this inspired spokesman would shortly observe: "Every thing shall be restored to its perfect frame, as it is now, or in the body, and shall be brought and be arraigned before the bar of *Christ the Son, and God the Father, and the Holy Spirit, which is one Eternal God,* to be judged according to their works."

At the same time, Jehovah is the one true God—the God known to men from the beginning. Zeezrom, anxious to trap the servant of the Lord, asked: "Who is he that shall come? Is it the Son of God?" Amulek appropriately replied, "Yea." His answer was perfect, and perfectly understandable to those with eyes of faith: Christ-Jehovah is both God and the Son of God, and, as we shall note in chapter nine, both Father and Son. The deceptive lawyer's questions simply provided a forum for the truth, an occasion for the declaration of deep and penetrating doctrine. Jehovah is the one true and living God, "the very Eternal Father of heaven and of earth." This God would come down to earth, take a body of flesh and bones, and offer salvation from sin to the truly repentant. (Alma 11:21-44, italics added.)[9]

Because men must believe this dimension of the "doctrine of Christ" in order to be saved—the doctrine that the premortal Lord Omnipotent would take a mortal and then an immortal body in working out the infinite and eternal atonement—Satan has labored incessantly to deny and stamp out the true message with regard to the coming of the Messiah. So it is that in the Nephite record we find repeatedly the haughty assertion of the anti-Christ: "There shall be no Christ!" Sherem (Jacob 7), Nehor (Alma 1), and Korihor (Alma 30) are among the most vocal and visible of the anti-Christs in the Book of Mormon. Skilled orators like Sherem and Korihor contended that things of the future (and, essentially, things of the Spirit) could not be known (Jacob 7:1-9; Alma 30:13-15, 24-26, 48).

There was also another group of anti-Christs who proved to be particularly interesting: the Zoramites. The Zoramites had, as a result of their false traditions and idolatry, rejected the law of Moses and the ordinances of the true Church. Alma and his missionary companions discovered that these people had "built synagogues, and that they did gather themselves together on one day of the week." The Nephite missionaries noted also that the Zoramites "had a place built up in the center of their synagogue, a place for standing" where each person would utter the same prayer. (Alma 31:1, 8-14.) The words of the prayer are most instructive in assessing the extent of their apostasy:

> Holy, holy God; we believe that thou art God, and we believe that thou art holy, and that thou wast a spirit, and that thou art a spirit, and that *thou wilt be a spirit forever.*
>
> Holy God, we believe that thou hast separated us from our brethren; and we do not believe in the tradition of our brethren, which was handed down to them by the childishness of their fathers; but we believe that thou hast elected us to be thy holy children; and also thou hast made it known unto us that there shall be no Christ. (Alma 31:15-16, italics added.)

This group of apostates seemed to be caught up in a type of predestination, a doctrine of unconditional election and reprobation. Most interesting for the purposes of our discussion, however, is the fact that they had come to deny the coming Messiah by denying the coming condescension and incarnation of Jehovah; stated simply, to say that their God would always be a spirit was equivalent to saying that there would be no Christ.

The belief that the Eternal God would come to earth as a mortal Messiah was often very unpopular among those who needed a Messiah most. Lehi bore witness to the people of Jerusalem of the need for repentance, and of the impending doom should spiritual change not take place. He also spoke of "the coming of a Messiah, and also the redemption of the world." Note the reaction of the people: "And when the Jews heard these things they were angry with him; yea, even as with the prophets of old, whom they had cast out, and stoned, and slain; and they also sought his life, that they might take it away." (1 Nephi 1:19-20; compare Alma 21:9-10.)[10] Limhi explained to Ammon concerning the wickedness of King Noah and the atrocities committed during his abominable reign:

> And a prophet of the Lord [Abinadi] have they slain; yea, a chosen man of God, who told them of their wickedness and abominations, and prophesied of many things which are to come, yea, even the coming of Christ.
>
> And because he said unto them that Christ was the God, the Father of all things, and said that he should take upon him the image of man, and it should be the image after which man was created in the beginning; or in other words, he said that man was created after the image of God, and that God should come down among the children of men, and take upon him flesh and blood, and go forth upon the face of the earth—
>
> And now, because he said this, they did put him to death. (Mosiah 7:26-28; compare 17:7-8.)

Conclusion

Christ was and is the Eternal God. The Lamb of God is also the one true Shepherd over all the earth, the Son of the Eternal Father, and the Savior of the world (1 Nephi 13:40-41). In the words of Nephi: "My soul delighteth in proving unto my people that save

Christ should come all men must perish. For if there be no Christ there be no God; and if there be no God we are not, for there could have been no creation. But there is a God, and he is Christ, and he cometh in the fulness of his own time." (2 Nephi 11:6-7.)

Notes

1. *Lectures on Faith* (Salt Lake City: Deseret Book Co., 1985), 2:2.

2. *Teachings of the Prophet Joseph Smith,* sel. Joseph Fielding Smith (Salt Lake City: Deseret Book Co., 1976), pp. 345-46.

3. *Man: His Origin and Destiny* (Salt Lake City: Deseret Book Co., 1954), p. 304.

4. *Doctrines of Salvation,* 3 vols., comp. Bruce R. McConkie (Salt Lake City: Bookcraft, 1954-56), 1:27; see also Joseph Fielding Smith, *Answers to Gospel Questions,* 5 vols., ed. Joseph Fielding Smith, Jr. (Salt Lake City: Deseret Book Co., 1957-66), 1:13-21; 3:58.

5. *Sermons and Writings of Bruce R. McConkie,* ed. Mark L. McConkie (Salt Lake City: Bookcraft, 1998), p. 64.

6. *The Promised Messiah* (Salt Lake City: Deseret Book Co., 1978), p. 98.

7. Joseph Smith taught that Christ had "descended in suffering below that which man can suffer; or, in other words, suffered greater sufferings, and was exposed to more powerful contradictions [compare Hebrews 12:3] than any man can be" (*Lectures on Faith* 5:2).

8. Elder Bruce R. McConkie has described the condescension of God as a dual matter: (1) the condescension of God the Father—Elohim; and (2) the condescension of God the Son—Christ (see *The Promised Messiah,* pp. 466-67; see also *The Mortal Messiah,* 4 vols. [Salt Lake City: Deseret Book Co., 1979-81], 1:314-15; *Mormon Doctrine,* 2d ed. [Salt Lake City: Bookcraft, 1966], p. 155).

9. For a brief discussion of the nature of the Godhead in the Book of Mormon (and specific reference to the encounter in Alma 11) see Roy W. Doxey, "I Have a Question," *Ensign,* August 1985, pp. 11-13.

10. Note in Alma 33:14-17 that the prophet Zenock was martyred because he had "testified of the Son of God, and because the people would not understand his words." See also Helaman 8:13-23.

He descended below all things, . . . that he might
be in all and through all things, the light of truth.
—D&C 88:6

7

Below All Things

*W*ho can comprehend the work of a God? What finite being is there that can fathom the ministerial labors of the Infinite One? It just may be that the members of the Church will never come to understand in this life the particulars of how it was that the Savior took upon him the effects of the sins of all mankind; how it was that Jesus of Nazareth engaged and bore the burden of all eternity; how it was that the Master descended below all things. But there are some things we do know. There are marvelous scriptural truths and prophetic utterances that shed a glorious light upon what was surely the greatest act of submission and love in all eternity. Though it is to modern revelation that we turn for doctrinal understanding concerning the mediation of Jesus Christ, it is upon the New Testament, the Gospels, that we rely for the details of the hours of atonement during our Lord's earthly ministry.

Having finished the Last Supper, the eleven Apostles, with Jesus at their head, left the upper room. Mark records: "When they had sung an hymn, they went out into the mount of Olives" (Mark 14:26). East of the temple mount, outside the walls of the Holy City, on the slopes of the Mount of Olives was a garden spot, a place where "Jesus ofttimes resorted . . . with his disciples" (John 18:2)—Gethsemane, the "garden of the oil press" (or winepress). A lifetime of purity and preparation was now a part of the past. The hour of ordeal, the major reason for which the great Jehovah had come to earth, was now at hand. It was a fateful occasion, transcendent in scope and incomprehensible to mortal minds; it was the hinge upon which the door into all eternity turned.

Assuming the Burden

"They came to a place which was named Gethsemane, which was a garden; and the disciples began to be sore amazed, and to be very heavy, and to complain in their hearts, wondering if this be the Messiah. And Jesus, knowing their hearts, said to his disciples, Sit ye here, while I pray." (JST, Mark 14:36-37.) As Elder Bruce R. McConkie has written: "Though they all knew, as Jesus himself attested in the private sermons and prayer just delivered [the Intercessory Prayer], that he was the Son of God, yet he did not fit the popular pattern for the Jewish Messiah, and the disciples, of course, had not yet received the gift of the Holy Ghost, which means they did not have the constant companionship of that member of the Godhead."[1] The time of anguish and alienation had begun. That for which the Lamb of God had been foreordained and that of which the prophets had spoken for millennia was under way. "When the unimaginable burden began to weigh upon Christ," Elder Neal A. Maxwell has taught, "it confirmed His long-held and intellectually clear understanding as to what He must now do."[2]

No weight is heavier than the burden of sin, and the Sinless One (and those closest to him) began to sense and feel the bitterness of this singular occasion, a time when the weight of the world was about to be placed upon the shoulders of him who had made the world. We must ever remember that Jesus was morally perfect. He had never taken a backward step or a moral detour. He was "in all points tempted like as we are, yet without sin" (Hebrews 4:15; compare 1 Peter 2:22). According to the Prophet Joseph Smith, Jesus was "the Son of God, and had the fullness of the Spirit, and greater power than any man."[3] He had never known the feelings of guilt and remorse, the pain of alienation from God that characterizes the whole of mankind.

There was a tragic aura surrounding this night of nights, when he who had always pleased the Father (John 8:29) and had thus never been alone (so far as being separated spiritually from his Father was concerned) was subjected to the forces and effects of sin that he had never known, forces that must have been poignantly and excruciatingly intense. The God of the fathers, the Holy One of Israel, the Lord God Omnipotent, as he was known among the ancients, knew all things (2 Nephi 9:20). And yet there was something he had never known personally: he had known neither sin nor its effects. Christ knew all things as a spirit being; "nevertheless," Alma taught, "the Son of God suffereth according to the flesh that he might take upon him the sins of his people, that he might blot out their transgressions according to the power of his deliverance" (Alma 7:13). In the words of Elder Maxwell, "The suffering Jesus began to be 'sore amazed' (Mark 14:33), or in the Greek, 'awestruck' and 'astonished.' Imagine, Jehovah, the Creator of this and other worlds, 'astonished'! Jesus knew cognitively what he must do, but not experientially. He had never personally known the exquisite and exacting process of an atonement before. Thus, when the agony came in its fulness, it was so much, much worse than even He with his unique intellect had ever imagined!"[4]

"He went forward a little, and fell on the ground, and prayed that, if it were possible, the hour might pass from him. And he said, Abba, Father, all things are possible unto thee; take away this cup from me: nevertheless not what I will, but what thou wilt." (Mark 14:35-36.) Removed from the Apostles "about a stone's cast" (Luke 22:41), the Master pleaded in prayer. He called out in tender tones, "Abba," an intimate and familiar form of *father,* perhaps something like what we know as "Daddy" or "Papa." Was there not another way, he asked? It did not appear so. Could the plan of salvation have been operative without Jesus' selfless submission to the torturous experiences of the hour? It would seem not. We have no scriptural or prophetic indication that some substitute savior waited in the wings, some person who could fill in should Jesus of Nazareth not complete the task at hand. We sing with conviction: "There was no other good enough to pay the price of sin. He only could unlock the gate of heaven and let us in."[5] No one else qualified for such an assignment. Earlier the Savior had spoken in soliloquy. "Now is my soul troubled," he had said, "and what shall I say? Father, save me from this hour: but for this cause came I unto this hour. Father, glorify thy name." The Father then spoke: "I have both glorified it, and will glorify it again." (John 12:27-28.)

Luke wrote: "There appeared an angel unto him from heaven, strengthening him. And being in an agony, he prayed more earnestly;

and he sweat as it were great drops of blood falling down to the ground." (JST, Luke 22:43-44.) An angel, sent from the courts of glory, came to strengthen the God of Creation in this hour of greatest need. "If we might indulge in speculation," Elder Bruce R. McConkie observed, "we would suggest that the angel who came into this second Eden was the same person who dwelt in the first Eden. At least Adam, who is Michael, the archangel—the head of the whole heavenly hierarchy of angelic ministrants—seems the logical one to give aid and comfort to his Lord on such a solemn occasion. Adam fell, and Christ redeemed men from the fall; theirs was a joint enterprise, both parts of which were essential for the salvation of the Father's children."[6]

Luke provided the additional detail concerning the intensity of our Lord's suffering—so great that drops of blood came to the surface of his body and fell to the ground. This was in fulfillment of the prophecy delivered by the angel to King Benjamin: "He shall suffer temptations, and pain of body, hunger, thirst, and fatigue, even more than man can suffer, except it be unto death; for behold, blood cometh from every pore, so great shall be his anguish for the wickedness and the abominations of his people" (Mosiah 3:7). In a modern revelation, the Savior pleaded with his people to repent, recalling the painful episode in Gethsemane:

> I command you to repent—repent, lest I smite you by the rod of my mouth, and by my wrath, and by my anger, and your sufferings be sore—how sore you know not, how exquisite you know not, yea, how hard to bear you know not.
>
> For behold, I, God, have suffered these things for all, that they might not suffer if they would repent;
>
> But if they would not repent they must suffer even as I;
>
> Which suffering caused myself, even God, the greatest of all, to tremble because of pain, and to bleed at every pore, and to suffer both body and spirit—and would that I might not drink the bitter cup, and shrink—
>
> Nevertheless, glory be to the Father, and I partook and finished my preparations unto the children of men. (D&C 19:15-18.)

The immediate consequence of sin is withdrawal of the Spirit (see Alma 34:35). It may be that such a withdrawal from an individual is what leads to feelings of guilt and pain and emptiness. Jesus Christ, in taking upon him the effects of the sins of all mankind, was thus exposed to the awful (and to Jesus, unusual) withdrawal of that Spirit that had been his constant companion from the beginning. In speaking of the atoning mission of Jesus Christ (and the ordeals related thereto), President Brigham Young explained:

> The Father withdrew His Spirit from His Son, at the time he was to be crucified. Jesus had been with his Father, talked with Him, dwelt in His bosom, and knew all about heaven, about making the earth, about the transgression of man, and what would redeem the people, and that he was the character who was to redeem the sons of earth, and the earth itself from all sin that had come upon it. The light, knowledge, power, and glory with which he was clothed were far above, or exceeded that of all others who had been upon the earth after the fall, consequently at the very moment, at the hour when the crisis came for him to offer up his life, the Father withdrew Himself, withdrew His Spirit. . . . That is what made him sweat blood. If he had had the power of God upon him, he would not have sweat blood.[7]

Concerning the suffering of Christ in Gethsemane, Elder James E. Talmage wrote:

> Christ's agony in the garden is unfathomable by the finite mind, both as to intensity and cause. The thought that He suffered through fear of death is untenable. Death to Him was preliminary to resurrection and triumphal return to the Father from whom He had come, and to a state of glory even beyond what He had before possessed; and, moreover, it was within His power to lay down His life voluntarily. He struggled and groaned under a burden such as no other being who has lived on earth might even conceive as possible. It was not physical pain, nor mental anguish alone, that caused Him to suffer such torture as to produce an extrusion of blood from every pore; but a spiritual agony of soul such as only God was capable of experiencing. No other man, however great his powers of physical or mental endurance, could have suffered so. . . . In some manner, actual and terribly real though to man incomprehensible, the Savior took upon Himself the burden of the sins of mankind from Adam to the end of the world.[8]

Just as ancient Israel had sent the scapegoat into the wilderness (Leviticus 16:5-10), even so the Lamb of God, suffering outside Jerusalem's walls and outside the pale of God's healing and redemptive

Spirit, met and faced the obstacles and assaults of Lucifer and his hosts. "In that hour of anguish Christ met and overcame all the horrors that Satan, 'the prince of this world,' could inflict. The frightful struggle incident to the temptations immediately following the Lord's baptism was surpassed and overshadowed by this supreme contest with the powers of evil."[9]

This was a night of irony. He who had come to impute righteousness to man's account had sin and evil imputed to his account. In Paul's words, God the Father had "made him to be sin for us, who knew no sin" (2 Corinthians 5:21). To the Galatian Saints, Paul also taught that "Christ hath redeemed us from the curse of the law, being made a curse for us" (Galatians 3:13). He who deserved least of all to suffer, now suffered most—more than mortal mind can fathom. He who had brought life—the more abundant life (John 10:10)—was subjected to the powers of death and darkness. As the Prophet Joseph Smith taught, Jesus Christ "descended in suffering below that which man can suffer; or, in other words, suffered greater sufferings, and was exposed to more powerful contradictions than any man can be."[10]

Through most of our Lord's infinite ordeal—which may have lasted for three or four hours[11]—the chief Apostles slept. It is almost impossible to imagine that these noble and obedient servants of the Lord, called to be special witnesses of his name in all the world, could not control the demands of the body for a brief moment—indeed, a moment that mattered. Elder McConkie has offered the following explanation: "Finite minds can no more comprehend how and in what manner Jesus performed his redeeming labors than they can comprehend how matter came into being, or how Gods began to be. Perhaps the very reason Peter, James, and John slept was to enable a divine providence to withhold from their ears, and seal up from their eyes, those things which only Gods can comprehend."[12]

Below All Things

Alma spoke with prophetic power when he described the coming of the Messiah and the suffering necessary to accomplish the Atonement:

He shall be born of Mary, at Jerusalem which is the land of our forefathers, she being a virgin, a precious and chosen vessel, who shall be overshadowed and conceive by the power of the Holy Ghost, and bring forth a son, yea, even the Son of God.

And he shall go forth, suffering pains and afflictions and temptations of every kind; and this that the word might be fulfilled which saith he will take upon him the pains and the sicknesses of his people.

And he will take upon him death, that he may loose the bands of death which bind his people; and he will take upon him their infirmities, that his bowels may be filled with mercy, according to the flesh, that he may know according to the flesh how to succor his people according to their infirmities. (Alma 7:10-12.)

In commenting upon these verses, Elder Neal A. Maxwell observed:

> Can we, even in the depths of disease, tell Him anything at all about suffering? In ways we cannot comprehend, our sicknesses and infirmities were borne by Him even before they were borne by us. The very weight of our combined sins caused Him to descend below all. We have never been, nor will we be, in depths such as He has known. Thus His atonement made perfect His empathy and His mercy and His capacity to succor us, for which we can be everlastingly grateful as He tutors us in our trials. There was no ram in the thicket at Calvary to spare Him, this Friend of Abraham and Isaac. . . .
>
> And when we feel so alone, can we presume to teach Him who trod "the wine-press alone" anything at all about feeling forsaken? . . .
>
> Should we seek to counsel Him in courage? Should we rush forth eagerly to show Him our press clippings and mortal medals—our scratches and bruises—as He bears His five special wounds? . . .
>
> Indeed, we cannot teach Him anything! But we can listen to Him. We can love Him; we can honor Him; we can worship Him. We can keep His commandments, and we can feast upon His scriptures.[13]

Conclusion

Thus our Savior descended below all things (see Ephesians 4:8-10; D&C 88:6). The Redeemer has indeed "trodden the wine-press alone, even the wine-press of the fierceness of the wrath of Almighty God" (D&C 76:107; 88:106; Isaiah 63:3). The miracle and blessings of the Atonement—timeless in their scope—continue to be extended to all who come to the Lord with righteous intent. "I am Christ," the Lord declared in a modern revelation, "and in mine own name, by the virtue of the blood which I have spilt, have I pleaded before the Father for them" (D&C 38:4). The nature of that pleading, that intercession, was elucidated some two months later in another revelation: "Listen to him who is the advocate with the Father, who is pleading your cause before him—saying: Father, behold the sufferings and death of him who did no sin, in whom thou wast well pleased; behold the blood of thy Son which was shed, the blood of him whom thou gavest that thyself might be glorified; wherefore, Father, spare these my brethren that believe on my name, that they may come unto me and have everlasting life" (D&C 45:3-5).

Notes

1. *The Mortal Messiah,* 4 vols. (Salt Lake City: Deseret Book Co., 1979-81), 4:123.

2. In Conference Report, April 1985, p. 92.

3. *Teachings of the Prophet Joseph Smith,* sel. Joseph Fielding Smith (Salt Lake City: Deseret Book Co., 1976), p. 188; compare JST, John 3:34.

4. In Conference Report, April 1985, p. 92.

5. "There Is a Green Hill Far Away," *Hymns,* no. 194.

6. *The Mortal Messiah* 4:125. See also Conference Report, April 1985, p. 10.

7. In *Journal of Discourses* (Liverpool: F. D. Richards & Sons, 1855-86), 3:206.

8. *Jesus the Christ* (Salt Lake City: Deseret Book Co., 1977), p. 613.

9. James E. Talmage, *Jesus the Christ,* p. 613.

10. *Lectures on Faith* (Salt Lake City: Deseret Book Co., 1985), 5:2.

11. See Bruce R. McConkie, in Conference Report, April 1985, p. 10.

12. *The Mortal Messiah* 4:124.

13. *Even As I Am* (Salt Lake City: Deseret Book Co., 1982), pp. 116-19.

It is expedient that there should be a great
and last sacrifice; . . . it shall not be a
human sacrifice; but it must be an
infinite and eternal sacrifice.
—*Alma 34:10*

8

Infinite and Eternal

The fall of Adam affected man, animals, and all forms of life on earth. Thus the redemption of man and earth must be as extensive as that fall. Adam brought mortality and death. The "Second Adam," Christ the Lord, brought immortality and eternal life. A blood fall required a blood atonement. A universal fall required a universal atonement. And such an act of reconciliation and intercession required the labors of one greater than man; it required the mediation of a God. The Atonement, like the Atoner, must be limitless and boundless; it must be infinite and eternal.

An Infinite Atonement

Elder B. H. Roberts taught that Adam's transgression was a transgression "against the majesty of God. Only a God can render a satisfaction to that insulted honor and majesty. Only Deity can satisfy the claims of Deity." He continued:

> Moreover the Atonement is not only a matter of satisfying the insulted honor and majesty of God adequately by like meeting like, and measure answering measure; but it is also a question of power. Not only must the dishonor towards God be removed by satisfaction, but there must be power over death; there must be a power of life that that

which was lost may be restored; and not only as to the spiritual life of man with God; but restored union between the spirit and body of man—physical life upon which the happiness and progress that God has designed for man depends. . . . As in Adam all die, so through the Redeemer of men must all be made alive, if the redemption is to be made complete. It was doubtless these considerations which led some of the Nephite prophets to say that the Atonement "must needs be an infinite atonement," by which, as I think, they sought to express the idea of the sufficiency of it; its completeness; the universality and power of it to restore all that was lost, both spiritual and physical, as well as to express the rank and dignity of him who would make the Atonement.

The Redeemer, then, must be a Lord of life, hence Deity. He must not only have the power of life within himself, but the power to impart it to others—a God-like power. . . . All these considerations lift the Redeemer and the Atonement far above man and what man can do. Truly the redemption of man is to be the work of God.[1]

With this substantive statement of Elder Roberts before us, let us consider some of the ways in which the atonement of Jesus Christ might be considered to be "infinite and eternal."

1. *The Atonement is timeless.* The atoning offering of our Lord is infinite and eternal in the sense that it is timeless—embracing past, present, and future. Our Savior is the Lamb "slain from the foundation of the world" (Revelation 13:8), and the effects of his atonement reach back to Eden and forward to the Millennium's end.[2] For example, Adam and Eve were taught to exercise faith in the name of the Son, a Savior who would suffer and die for the sins of mankind some four thousand years later (Moses 5:8). Adam learned directly from God himself that even as one is born into this mortal world by flesh and blood and spirit, so also must one be born again into the divine realm by entering the waters of baptism, by virtue of the cleansing blood of Christ, and through the medium of the Holy Spirit. Adam was thereafter baptized by immersion, was born of the Spirit, and became a son of God. (Moses 6:59, 64-68.)

Adam is but a pattern, an example. He typifies the ancients: they believed in Christ, just as we do. They repented of their sins, just as we do. They partook of the divine nature and through the Atonement became perfect in their generation, just as we are striving to do today. The Nephite record-keeper Jarom explained that "the prophets, and the priests, and the teachers, did labor diligently, exhorting with all long-suffering the people to diligence; teaching the law of Moses, and the intent for which it was given; persuading them to look forward unto the Messiah, and believe in him to come as though he already was" (Jarom 1:11; compare Mosiah 3:13). In counseling his errant son Corianton, Alma said: "And now I will ease your mind somewhat on this subject. Behold, you marvel why these things [the coming of Christ] should be known so long beforehand. Behold, I say unto you, is not a soul at this time as precious unto God as a soul will be at the time of his coming? Is it not as necessary that the plan of redemption should be made known unto this people as well as unto their children? Is it not as easy at this time for the Lord to send his angel to declare these glad tidings unto us as unto our children, or as after the time of his coming?" (Alma 39:17-19; compare D&C 20:21-27.)

Those who lived before Christ and who uttered messianic prophecies, as well as those who have lived since his mortal ministry and thus bear messianic testimonies, join in shouts of praise to the King Immanuel and offer humble but never-ending gratitude to him who has bought us with his blood.

2. *The Atonement overcomes death.* The Atonement is infinite in the sense that it confronts and conquers the most universal reality in this phase of our existence—death. All things are subject to death as a result of the Fall, and thus the light of the Atonement must shine upon all who are shadowed by the effects of that fall. Jacob wrote with power: "For as death hath passed upon all men, to fulfil the merciful plan of the great Creator, there must needs be a power of resurrection. . . . Wherefore, it must needs be an infinite atonement—save it should be an infinite atonement this corruption [corrupt and decaying body] could not put on incorruption [immortality]. Wherefore, the first judgment which came upon man must needs have remained to an endless duration. And if so, this flesh must have laid down to rot and to crumble to its mother earth, to rise no more." (2 Nephi 9:6-7.)

3. *Christ redeems all that he creates.* The Atonement is infinite in the sense that our Savior—the creator of worlds without number (Moses 7:30)—is also the redeemer of worlds without number. After having seen a vision of the earth and all its inhabitants, Moses asked the Lord two questions—why he had created the worlds, and how he

had done so. The Lord's answer to the first was that he had done so "for mine own purpose," which purpose he later made known: "For behold, this is my work and my glory—to bring to pass the immortality and eternal life of man." The answer to the second question—how he had created the worlds—was given as follows: "By the word of my power, have I created them, which is mine Only Begotten Son, who is full of grace and truth. And worlds without number have I created; and I also created them for mine own purpose; and by the Son I created them, which is mine Only Begotten." The Lord then explained to Moses: "But only an account of this earth, and the inhabitants thereof, give I unto you. For behold, there are many worlds that have passed away by the word of my power. And there are many that now stand, and innumerable are they unto man; but all things are numbered unto me, for they are mine and I know them." (Moses 1:30-35, 39.)

In Joseph Smith's vision of the glories, the Prophet learned that by Christ, "and through him, and of him, the worlds are and were created, and the inhabitants thereof are begotten sons and daughters unto God" (D&C 76:24; compare vv. 40-42). From this we can infer that on the other worlds which the Master has created—even as it is here on our earth—men and women come unto Christ, receive his gospel and saving ordinances, put off the natural man, and are born again unto that life that pertains to the Spirit. They become, first of all, sons and daughters of Christ; then, continuing to mature in the ways of righteousness until they become joint heirs, co-inheritors, with Christ to all that the Father has, they become the sons and daughters of God, meaning the Father.[3]

In 1843 the Prophet Joseph Smith prepared a poetic version of the vision. The verses associated with the above passage read as follows:

> And I heard a great voice, bearing record from heav'n,
> He's the Saviour, and only begotten of God—
> By him, of him, and through him, the worlds were all made,
> Even all that career in the heavens so broad,
> Whose inhabitants, too, from the first to the last,
> Are sav'd by the very same Saviour of ours;
> And, of course, are begotten God's daughters and sons,
> By the very same truths, and the very same pow'rs.[4]

4. *Christ is an infinite being.* The atonement of Jesus Christ is infinite because he who wrought the atonement is himself infinite and eternal. From his mother, Mary—a mortal woman—he inherited mortality, the capacity to die. On the other hand, he inherited from his Father, the Almighty Elohim, immortality, the power to live forever. The suffering and sacrifice in Gethsemane and on Golgotha were undertaken by a being who was greater than man, one possessing the powers of a God. This was no human sacrifice, nor even simply the act of a wise and all-loving teacher. It was more, infinitely more, than an example of submission or a model of humanitarianism. He did for us what no other being could do.

An angel explained to King Benjamin that Jesus would "suffer temptations, and pain of body, hunger, thirst, and fatigue, *even more than man can suffer,* except it be unto death. . . . And lo, he cometh unto his own, that salvation might come unto the children of men even through faith on his name; and even after all this *they shall consider him a man,* and say that he hath a devil, and shall scourge him, and shall crucify him." (Mosiah 3:7, 9, italics added.) Amulek similarly spoke of Christ's redemptive labors:

> For it is expedient that an atonement should be made; for according to the great plan of the Eternal God there must be an atonement made, or else all mankind must unavoidably perish; yea, all are hardened; yea, all are fallen and are lost, and must perish except it be through the atonement which it is expedient should be made.
>
> For it is expedient that there should be a great and last sacrifice; yea, not a sacrifice of man, neither of beast, neither of any manner of fowl; for it shall not be a human sacrifice; but it must be an infinite and eternal sacrifice.
>
> Now there is not any man that can sacrifice his own blood which will atone for the sins of another. Now, if a man murdereth, behold will our law, which is just, take the life of his brother? I say unto you, Nay.
>
> But the law requireth the life of him who hath murdered; therefore there can be nothing which is short of an infinite atonement which will suffice for the sins of the world.

Amulek then explained that this "great and last sacrifice" would bring to an end the shedding of the blood of animals in sacrificial similitude. And then he said, "This is the whole meaning of the law [of Moses], every whit pointing to that great and last sacrifice; and that great and last sacrifice will be *the Son of God, yea, infinite and eternal.*" (Alma 34:9-12, 14, italics added.)

"If the Flesh Should Rise No More . . ."

Some profound truths are best understood in paradox. For example, Jesus Christ's sacrifice was a voluntary one—he chose to offer up himself; his was a willing sacrifice. On the other hand, to fulfil God's plan it was absolutely necessary, as Amulek mentioned (above), that an atonement be made, that a God come to earth, experience the pulls and perils of mortality, suffer infinitely during the hours of atonement, die, and rise again from the tomb. It had to be. There was no other option. And Christ had to be the one to do it; his sacrifice, therefore, was crucial. But what if there had been no atonement? What if Christ had refused to imbibe the bitter cup in Gethsemane? Because the ransom has been paid, because the gift has been offered, today we are able to speak of the question only hypothetically. The ancient prophets, however, spoke in ways that dramatized the absolute necessity and indispensability of the Atonement.

Nephi gloried in his Redeemer: "My soul delighteth in proving unto my people that save Christ should come all men must perish." And then, in arguing toward the absurd, he continued: "For if there be no Christ there be no God; and if there be no God we are not, for there could have been no creation. But there is a God, and he is Christ, and he cometh in the fulness of his own time." (2 Nephi 11:6-7; compare 2:11-13.)

Alma did precisely the same thing in his fatherly counsel to Corianton. To illustrate that mercy cannot rob justice, that unrepentant sin cannot go unpunished, that the Redeemer is a God of justice as well as a God of mercy, and that the Atonement requires both, Alma explained: "According to justice, the plan of redemption could not be brought about, only on conditions of repentance of men in this probationary state, yea, this preparatory state; for except it were for these conditions, mercy could not take effect except it should destroy the work of justice. Now the work of justice could not be destroyed; if so, God would cease to be God." Further, "there is a law given, and a punishment affixed, and a repentance granted; which repentance, mercy claimeth; otherwise, justice claimeth the creature and executeth the law, and the law inflicteth the punishment; if not so, the works of justice would be destroyed, and God would cease to be God." (Alma 42:13, 22.)

God cannot and will not cease to be God. His title, his status, and his exalted position are forever fixed and immutable. Nor need the Saints of God spend a particle of a second worrying and fretting about the Almighty falling from grace. Joseph Smith explained in the Lectures on Faith (lecture 4) that for the Saints to do so is to err in doctrine as to the true nature of God and thus fall short of that dynamic faith that leads to life and salvation. Alma's hypothetical case is just that—purely hypothetical. He is arguing toward the impossible, the absurd, to emphasize the logical certainty of the principle that mercy cannot rob justice. It is as if Alma had said: "It is as ridiculous to suppose that mercy can rob justice and that men and women can break the laws of God with impunity, as it is to suppose that God can cease to be God." In fact, Alma concludes: "God ceaseth not to be God, and mercy claimeth the penitent, and mercy cometh because of the atonement" (Alma 42:23).

Abinadi observed that "if Christ had not come into the world, speaking of things to come as though they had already come, there could have been no redemption. And if Christ had not risen from the dead, or have broken the bands of death that the grave should have no victory, and that death should have no sting, there could have been no resurrection." (Mosiah 16:6-7.) It is to Jacob, however, that we go for a more thorough treatment of this topic. In singing the song of redeeming love, Jacob expressed gratitude for his Master: "O the wisdom of God," he said, "his mercy and grace! For behold, if the flesh should rise no more"—that is, if Christ had not risen from the dead and thus the bodies of all men would remain in the graves— "our spirits must become subject to that angel who fell from before the presence of the Eternal God, and became the devil, to rise no more. And our spirits must have become like unto him, and we become devils, angels to a devil, to be shut out from the presence of our God, and to remain with the father of lies, in misery, like unto himself." (2 Nephi 9:8-9.)

Why? Why, if there were no resurrection, would a person after his physical death remain in the spirit world, be subject to Satan, and eventually become like Satan? Would this also be true of a good man, one who had lived a moral and upright life?

The Resurrection was the physical evidence of Christ's divine sonship, the outward proof that he was indeed the Son of the Everlasting Father, the Messiah. If Jesus did not have the power to rise from the tomb, power to save the body—as he said he did—then he did not have power to forgive sins, to save the soul. This is what Paul meant when he wrote to the Corinthians that "if Christ be not risen, then is our preaching vain, and your faith is also vain. . . . And if Christ be not raised, your faith is vain; ye are yet in your sins." (1 Corinthians 15:14, 17.) The fact is, "all have sinned, and come short of the glory of God" (Romans 3:23). No person will traverse life's roads without some spiritual detour. Therefore if there had been no redemption from physical death through the resurrection, there would be no redemption from sin and spiritual death; we would remain in our sins—unclean, impure, and unprotected from the buffetings and ultimate conquest of the arch-deceiver. We would degenerate from righteousness and become like the enemy of righteousness. "Our spirits, stained with sin, unable to cleanse themselves, would be subject to the author of sin everlastingly; we would be followers of Satan; we would be sons of perdition."[5]

But thanks be to God—there is an atonement! Relief and recovery and reclamation are realities. Deliverance is within reach and hope is realizable. "Know this," Elder Boyd K. Packer testified, "Truth, glorious truth, proclaims there is . . . a Mediator. 'For there is one God, and one mediator between God and men, the man Christ Jesus' (1 Timothy 2:5). Through Him mercy can be fully extended to each of us without offending the eternal law of justice. This truth is the very root of Christian doctrine. You may know much about the gospel as it branches out from there, but if you only know the branches and those branches do not touch that root, if they have been cut free from that truth, there will be no life nor substance nor redemption in them."[6] Truly, "How great, how glorious, how complete, redemption's grand design, where justice, love, and mercy meet in harmony divine!"[7]

Conclusion

The Saints rejoice in the fact that Christ "hath abolished death, and hath brought life and immortality to light through the gospel" (2 Timothy 1:10). The medicine must be sufficiently strong to cure the malady, the antidote at least equal to the toxin. The transgression of our first parents brought sin and death to all who would inhabit planet Earth. The suffering and death and resurrection of the Lord Jesus brought justification and life to all who will receive it (see Romans 5:12-18). "If it were not for the plan of redemption, (laying it aside) as soon as they were dead their souls were miserable, being cut off from the presence of the Lord" (Alma 42:11). Christ and his atonement are infinite and eternal; through the power of God misery is transformed into happiness, death into life eternal.

Notes

1. *The Seventy's Course in Theology: Fourth Year—The Atonement* (Dallas, Texas: Reprinted by S. K. Taylor Publishing Company, 1976), pp. 94-95.

2. Elder Orson Pratt believed the scriptural statement that Christ was the Lamb slain from the foundation of the world to be an allusion to the manner in which the Atonement operated in the premortal world to forgive sin in that pristine existence. "The very fact," he wrote in 1853, "that the atonement which was to be made in a future world, was considered as already having been made, seems to show that there were those who had sinned, and who stood in need of the atonement. The nature of the sufferings of Christ was such that it could redeem the spirits of men as well as their bodies. . . . All the spirits when they come here are innocent, that is, if they have ever committed sins, they have repented and obtained forgiveness through faith in the future sacrifice of the Lamb." (*The Seer* [Washington, D.C., April 1853], vol. 1, no. 4, pp. 54, 56.)

3. See Robert L. Millet and Joseph Fielding McConkie, *In His Holy Name* (Salt Lake City: Bookcraft, 1988), pp. 21-22.

4. *Times and Seasons,* 6 vols. (Nauvoo, Illinois: The Church of Jesus Christ of Latter-day Saints, 1839-46), 4:82-83.

5. Bruce R. McConkie, *A New Witness for the Articles of Faith* (Salt Lake City: Deseret Book Co., 1985), p. 130.

6. In Conference Report, April 1977, p. 80.

7. "How Great the Wisdom and the Love," *Hymns,* no. 195.

*Behold, I am Jesus Christ. I am the Father and
the son. In me shall all mankind have life,
and that eternally, even they who shall
believe on my name.*
—Ether 3:14

9

The Father and the Son

*I*n our quest to know and understand the Lord Jesus, we inevitably come face to face with the eternal fact that he is more than a loving friend, more than a noble example, even more than our Elder Brother. He has met and conquered Satan; descended below all mortal stresses and challenges; and risen from the grave to inherit glorious immortality and the fulness of the glory of the Father. Therefore God "hath highly exalted him, and given him a name which is above every name: that at the name of Jesus every knee should bow, of things in heaven, and things in earth, and things under the earth; and that every tongue should confess that Jesus Christ is Lord, to the glory of God the Father" (Philippians 2:9-11).

The Name of Christ Known Anciently

Jacob, the brother of Nephi, rejoiced in the assurance he had that his posterity would eventually come to "the true knowledge of their Redeemer." He continued: "Wherefore, as I said unto you, it must needs be expedient that Christ—for in the last night the angel spake unto me that this should be his name—should come among the Jews, among those who are the more wicked part of the world." (2 Nephi 10:2-3.) It is difficult to know exactly what Jacob had in mind in the preceding statement. Did he not know before this time that the name of the Holy One of Israel would be Christ? Did he mean that the angel had simply confirmed in his mind the specific name of the Messiah, something he already knew? The question here is largely one of language: we know the Lord Jehovah as Jesus Christ, names that literally mean, respectively, "the Lord is salvation" and "the Messiah" or "the Anointed One." The exact name by which Christ was known to other peoples of the past (and of different languages) is unknown to us. Elder Theodore M. Burton has written by way of explanation:

> We do not know the language or the exact words used by the Book of Mormon prophets. Certainly they did not speak English. A good translator translates meanings and not just words. The reader of the translation must be able to understand the thought expressed in the original work and understand the meaning thereof. If Joseph Smith, in translating the words actually used, had written down the original words, no one would have understood what was meant. Even if he had used the English equivalents and had written "the Redeemer, the Anointed," not everyone would have understood whom he referred to. But when he translated those words as *Jesus Christ,* everyone understood, and that very quickly. It is a good translation. . . .
>
> Thus, the ancient Book of Mormon prophets and the prophets of the Old Testament were all speaking of the same person, though they used the words their people would understand. They referred to the same person we refer to as "Jesus Christ, the Son of God." Regardless of the language they used, the meaning is clear. Joseph Smith, in translating the Book of Mormon, used the words "Jesus Christ" because they gave a clear-cut understanding of what was written by the original scribe.[1]

Nephi similarly spoke of the coming of the Anointed One, bearing a confirmatory witness (of that of his prophetic predecessors and of the word of angels): "For according to the words of the prophets, the Messiah cometh in six hundred years from the time that my father left Jerusalem; and according to the words of the prophets, and also the word of the angel of God, his name shall be Jesus Christ, the Son of God" (2 Nephi 25:19). The angel who explained to King Benjamin the condescension of God attested to His infinite anguish and suffering. The angel then taught, "And he shall be called Jesus Christ, the Son of God, . . . and his mother shall be called Mary" (Mosiah 3:8). Even as Adam was counseled by an angel to do all that he did in the name of the Son (Moses 5:8), so the prophets have affirmed that "as the Lord God liveth, there is none other name given under heaven save it be this Jesus Christ, of which [has been] spoken, whereby man can be saved" (2 Nephi 25:20; compare 31:21; Mosiah 3:17; Moses 6:52; Acts 4:12).

Father by Creation

Elohim is the Father of the spirits of all men, including that of Jesus Christ (Hebrews 12:9; Numbers 16:22), and is thus the ultimate object of our worship. "True worshipers," Jesus taught the woman at the well in Samaria, "shall worship the Father in spirit and in truth; for the Father seeketh such to worship him" (JST, John 4:25). Elohim is our Father because he gave us life—provided a spirit birth for each of us. Jesus Christ is also known by the title of Father, and is so designated in scripture.[2] We will now consider some of the ways in which the Lord Jehovah—Jesus the Christ—is called Father.

Jesus Christ is known as Father by virtue of his role as Creator. Long before he became mortal he was directly involved in creation. "While yet in the premortal existence Jehovah advanced and progressed until he became like unto God. Under the direction of the Father he became the Creator of worlds without number, and thus was himself the Lord Omnipotent."[3] Enoch expressed the grandeur of the Lord's creative enterprise when he exclaimed: "Were it possible that man could number the particles of the earth, yea, millions of earths like this, it would not be a beginning to the number of thy creations" (Moses 7:30). To Moses the Lord explained: "By the word of my power, have I created [the worlds], which is mine Only Begotten Son, who is full of grace and truth. And worlds without number have I created; and I also created them for mine own purpose; and by the Son I created them, which is mine Only Begotten." (Moses 1:31-33; compare Hebrews 1:1-3.)

Because Jehovah-Christ created the heavens and the earth, he is appropriately known in the Book of Mormon as "the Father of heaven and of earth." The Nephite and Jaredite prophets came to know full well that the Messiah, the Only Begotten Son of the Father in the flesh, was the same being who had created all things (see 2 Nephi 25:12). The angel explained to King Benjamin that "he shall be called Jesus Christ, the Son of God, the Father of heaven and earth, the Creator of all things from the beginning" (Mosiah 3:8).

Zeezrom asked Amulek: "Is the Son of God the very Eternal Father? And Amulek said unto him: Yea, he is the very Eternal Father of heaven and of earth, and all things which in them are; he is the beginning and the end, the first and the last." (Alma 11:38-39.) Prior to his ministry to the Nephites, and immediately following the destruction in the New World, Jehovah spoke: "Behold, I am Jesus Christ the Son of God. I created the heavens and the earth, and all things that in them are. I was with the Father from the beginning. I am in the Father, and the Father in me; and in me hath the Father glorified his name." (3 Nephi 9:15.)

Father Through Spiritual Rebirth

As the Savior and foreordained Messiah, Jesus Christ became "the author of eternal salvation unto all them that obey him" (Hebrews 5:9), and the Father's gospel, the gospel of God (Romans 1:1), became his by adoption—the gospel of Jesus Christ. Jesus became the advocate and intercessor for fallen man, the way to the Father (see John 14:6). Under the Almighty Elohim, Jehovah became the Father of Salvation, the Father of eternal life (see Ether 3:14).

Those on earth who accept the gospel of Jesus Christ enter the family of Jesus Christ, take upon them the family name, and thus become inheritors of family obligations and family privileges. Inasmuch as one was not originally a member of the family of the Lord Jesus prior to the time of accountability (or conversion), he must be adopted into that family; one must "subscribe the articles of adoption," must have faith in Christ, repent of all sins, be baptized by immersion by a legal administrator, and receive and enjoy the gift of the Holy Ghost—meet the legal requirements of the kingdom of God—to properly qualify and be received into the new family relationship.[4]

Spiritual rebirth is an absolute necessity for one who aspires to the celestial kingdom. Even as one may enter mortality only through mortal birth, so also may one qualify for life in the spiritual realm— eternal life—only after spiritual rebirth, through being born again as to things of righteousness. The Lord commanded Adam to teach these things freely unto his children, saying "that by reason of transgression cometh the fall, which fall bringeth death, and inasmuch as ye were born into the world by water, and blood, and the spirit, which I have made, and so became of dust a living soul, even so ye must be born again into the kingdom of heaven, of water, and of the Spirit, and be cleansed by blood, even the blood of mine Only Begotten; that ye might be sanctified from all sin, and enjoy the words of eternal life in this world, and eternal life in the world to come, even immortal glory" (Moses 6:59).

Jesus Christ becomes the covenant Father of all who receive and abide by the terms and conditions of his new and everlasting covenant, the fulness of his gospel (D&C 66:2; 133:57). That person who enters the gospel covenant and strives thereafter to live worthy of the directions and purifying powers of the Spirit is born again into this new family relationship; he becomes "as a child" in the sense of becoming "submissive, meek, humble, patient, full of love, willing to submit to all things which the Lord seeth fit to inflict upon him, even as a child doth submit to his father" (Mosiah 3:19). As it is with the physical creation of the heavens and the earth, so it is with the human character and personality: Christ is the Father of creation, and through applying his atoning blood men and women become "new creations," "new creatures in Christ" (see Mosiah 27:26) through the medium of the Holy Ghost.

After a stirring and inspiring sermon by their noble king and spiritual leader, Benjamin, the Nephites were so overcome by the Spirit of the Lord that they had "no more disposition to do evil, but to do good continually" (Mosiah 5:2). Further, they entered into a sacred covenant to keep the commandments of God all the remainder of their days. King Benjamin was delighted by the people's response and added, "And now, because of the covenant which ye have made ye shall be called the children of Christ, his sons, and his daughters; for behold, this day he hath spiritually begotten you; for ye say that your hearts are changed through faith on his name; therefore, ye are born of him and have become his sons and his daughters." Benjamin then enjoined upon his people the responsibility to take upon them the family name—the name of Christ—that they might know both the voice and the name by which the Lord could eventually call them home (Mosiah 5:1-15).

Abinadi challenged the life-styles of wicked King Noah and his priests. In the process of delivering a scathing denunciation, he also delivered a penetrating commentary on Isaiah's greatest messianic utterance (Isaiah 53). Isaiah had said of the coming Messiah, "When thou shalt make his soul an offering for sin, he shall see his seed" (Isaiah 53:10). Abinadi explained:

> Behold I say unto you, that whosoever has heard the words of the prophets, yea, all the holy prophets who have prophesied concerning the coming of the Lord—I say unto you, that all those who have hearkened unto their words, and believed that the Lord would redeem his people, and have looked forward to that day for a remission of their sins, I say unto you, that these are his seed, or they are the heirs of the kingdom of God.
>
> For these are they whose sins he has borne; these are they for whom he has died, to redeem them from their transgressions. And now, are they not his seed? (Mosiah 15:11-12.)

When he had finished his work on Calvary, the Lord of the living and the dead entered the world of spirits. Having made his soul "an offering for sin" in Gethsemane and on the cross, the Master was greeted in the spirit world by his seed, "an innumerable company of the spirits of the just," the righteous dead from the days of Adam to the meridian of time. He taught these persons—his seed—the principles of his gospel and prepared them to come forth in a glorious resurrection. (See D&C 138:12-19.)[5]

Finally, let us consider the words of Christ himself to the Nephites prior to his visit to America: "I came unto my own, and my own received me not. And the scriptures concerning my coming are fulfilled. And as many as have received me, to them have I given to become the sons of God; and even so will I to as many as shall believe on my name, for behold, by me redemption cometh, and in me is the law of Moses fulfilled." (3 Nephi 9:16-17; compare Ether 3:14.)

Father by Divine Investiture of Authority

Jesus explained to a group during his Palestinian ministry: "I am come in my Father's name" (John 5:43). Our Lord acted and spoke on behalf of Elohim, hence he could proclaim, "My doctrine is not mine, but his that sent me" (John 7:16). Christ is therefore known as Father "by divine investiture of authority,"[6] meaning that "the Father-Elohim has placed his name upon the Son, has given him his own power and authority, and has authorized him to speak in the first person as though he were the original or primal Father."[7]

In numerous instances throughout the standard works we can see this principle in operation. "And [Jehovah] called upon our father Adam by his own voice, saying: I am God; I made the world, and men before they were in the flesh. And he also said unto him: If thou wilt turn unto me, and hearken unto my voice, and believe, and repent of all thy transgressions, and be baptized, even in water, in the name of mine Only Begotten Son, who is full of grace and truth, which is Jesus Christ, the only name which shall be given under heaven, whereby salvation shall come unto the children of men, ye shall receive the gift of the Holy Ghost." (Moses 6:51-52.)

To Enoch the Lord spoke: "And that which I have chosen [the Savior] hath pled before my face. Wherefore, he suffereth for their sins; inasmuch as they will repent in the day that my Chosen shall return unto me, and until that day they [those in "prison" in the spirit world] shall be in torment; wherefore, for this shall the heavens weep, yea, and all the workmanship of mine hands." (Moses 7:39-40.)

Another occasion on which the premortal Christ spoke on behalf of his Father is found in the experience of Moses on an unnamed mountain. Jehovah said, "My works are without end, and also my words, for they never cease." And then he continued: "And I have a work for thee, Moses, my son; and thou art in the similitude of mine Only Begotten; and mine Only Begotten is and shall be the Savior, for he is full of grace and truth." (Moses 1:4, 6; compare vv. 32-33.)[8]

We find the principle of divine investiture of authority particularly prevalent in the Doctrine and Covenants. In fact, there are a number of occasions on which the Lord has chosen to speak as both Christ and Elohim in the same revelation. For example, in section 29 of the Doctrine and Covenants we read the following verse: "Listen to the voice of Jesus Christ, your Redeemer, the Great I AM, whose arm of mercy hath atoned for your sins" (D&C 29:1). But now note verse 42 of the same section: "I, the Lord God, gave unto Adam and unto his seed, that they should not die as to the temporal death, until I, the Lord God, should send forth angels to declare unto them repentance and redemption, through faith on the name of mine Only Begotten Son."

In Doctrine and Covenants 49 the same principle is at work, this time in the other direction. "Thus saith the Lord; for I am God, and have sent mine Only Begotten Son into the world for the redemption of the world" (v. 5). Now note the last verse of the revelation: "Behold, I am Jesus Christ, and I come quickly" (D&C 49:28). What better way to establish firmly in the minds of the Saints that the words of Jehovah are the words of Elohim; that they have the same mind and thoughts; that they are totally and completely one?[9]

The Book of Mormon demonstrates investiture of authority in yet other ways than those we have considered so far. One of the powerful witnesses of the Nephite and Jaredite records is that Jesus Christ is Father because Elohim has literally invested his Son with his own attributes and powers. In the words of Elder Bruce R. McConkie: "How is our Lord the Father? It is because of the atonement, because he received power from his Father to do that which is infinite and eternal. This is a matter of his Eternal Parent investing him with power from on high so that he becomes the Father because he exercises the power of that Eternal Being."[10] In like manner, President John Taylor wrote that Christ "is also called the Very Eternal Father. Does not this mean that in Him were the attributes and power of the very Eternal Father?"[11]

One of the most penetrating sermons ever delivered was Abinadi's defense before King Noah and his wicked priests. The doctrine of this sermon is deep and profound. Abinadi had just quoted from Isaiah's great messianic prophecy (Isaiah 53):

> And now Abinadi said unto them: I would that ye should understand that God himself shall come down among the children of men, and shall redeem his people.
> And because he dwelleth in flesh he shall be called the Son of God, and having subjected the flesh to the will of the Father, being the Father and the Son—
> The Father, because he was conceived by the power of God; and the Son, because of the flesh; thus becoming the Father and the Son—
> And they are one God, yea, the very Eternal Father of heaven and of earth. (Mosiah 15:1-4.)

A number of key doctrinal matters are given in the foregoing text:

1. God himself—Jehovah, the God of ancient Israel—would come to earth, take a body of flesh and bones, and accomplish the work of redemption for all mankind.

2. Because Jehovah-Christ would have a physical body and dwell in the flesh—like every other mortal son and daughter of God—he would be known as the *Son* of God. At the same time, because he would be conceived by the power of God, and would thus have within him the powers of the *Spirit,* he would be known as the *Father.* In a modern revelation given in 1833, the Savior explained to the Prophet Joseph Smith that he is "the Father because he [Elohim] gave me of his fulness, and the Son because I was in the world and made flesh my tabernacle, and dwelt among the sons of men." Christ is thus known as the Son of God; in mortality his growth and development—like that of all the sons and daughters of God—were gradual, taking place line upon line and precept upon precept. That is, he received "grace for grace" and continued "from grace to grace" until he eventually received in the Resurrection a fulness of the glory of the Father. "And thus he was called the Son of God, because he received not of the fulness at the first." (D&C 93:4, 12-14.)

3. The will of the Son was to be swallowed up in the will of the Father. That is, the flesh would become subject to the Spirit, the mortal subject to the immortal. "I seek not mine own will," Jesus explained, "but the will of the Father which hath sent me" (John 5:30). Also, "I came down from heaven, not to do mine own will, but the will of him that sent me" (John 6:38). In short, Jesus would do what Elohim would have him do.

4. Thus Christ would be both the Father and the Son. He would be called the Father because he was conceived by the power of God and inherited all of the divine endowments, particularly immortality, from his exalted sire. He would be called the Son because of his flesh—his mortal inheritance from his mother, Mary. Therefore, Christ would be both flesh and spirit, both man and God, both Son and Father. And they—the Father and the Son, the God and the man, the spirit and the flesh—are to be blended wondrously in one being, Jesus Christ, "the very Eternal Father of heaven and of earth." Indeed, the Book of Mormon is an additional witness that in Christ "dwelleth all the fulness of the Godhead bodily" (Colossians 2:9).

A final matter that might be mentioned briefly is the manner in which Christ spoke repeatedly of Elohim the Father during his Nephite ministry. On these occasions Jesus ascribed his words to Elohim, which, as we have noted already, are also the words and feelings of Jehovah. He spoke of the doctrine of the Father (3 Nephi

11:31-32); the law and commandments of the Father (3 Nephi 12:19); the Father granting the land of America as an inheritance (3 Nephi 15:13; 16:16); the Father making covenants with Abraham and the house of Israel (3 Nephi 16:5; 20:27); the mercies and judgments of the Father (3 Nephi 16:9); and the words given by the Father to Malachi (3 Nephi 24:1). Christ here showed deference and total commitment to Elohim, for the Lord Jesus also made clear to the Nephites that he (Christ) was the God of ancient Israel, the God who made covenant with Abraham, the God who gave the law of Moses, the God of the whole earth (3 Nephi 11:14; 15:5). As we have sought to establish, the words of one (Jehovah-Christ) are the words of the other (Elohim), and thus reference to the Father will frequently include (and intend) reference to both Elohim and the premortal Jesus Christ.

Conclusion

Less than two months before his death, Joseph Smith said to the Saints in Nauvoo: "The Savior has the words of eternal life. Nothing else can profit us." He then counseled his people, "I advise all to go on to perfection, and search deeper and deeper into the mysteries of Godliness."[12] One of the greatest mysteries in the Christian world is the matter of the Godhead, the relationship of the Father and the Son. If it is truly life eternal to know God and his Son (John 17:3; D&C 132:24), then surely God does not seek to remain unknown, nor to have his children glory in the mystery of his incomprehensibility. As the modern seer taught in 1844, "It is the first principle of the gospel to know for a certainty the character of God."[13] Thus we conclude that the first principle of revealed religion centers in God— who he is, how he is related to Jesus Christ, and what we must do to know and be like them.

God has revealed himself anew in our day. But the "restitution of all things" is still under way, and the doctrinal restoration (certainly including many more truths concerning God and his nature) will continue into the Millennium.[14]

> God shall give unto you knowledge by his Holy Spirit, yea, by the unspeakable gift of the Holy Ghost, that has not been revealed since the world was until now;

Which our forefathers have awaited with anxious expectation to be revealed in the last times, which their minds were pointed to by the angels, as held in reserve for the fulness of their glory;

A time to come in the which nothing shall be withheld, whether there be one God or many gods, they shall be manifest.

All thrones and dominions, principalities and powers, shall be revealed and set forth upon all who have endured valiantly for the gospel of Jesus Christ. (D&C 121:26-29.)

Until that glorious day, we have available to us priceless volumes of scripture which contain a veritable flood of intelligence regarding the nature of God and particularly the ministry of the Father and the Son. "And now," the prophet Moroni beckoned, "I would commend you to seek this Jesus of whom the prophets and apostles have written, that the grace of God the Father, and also the Lord Jesus Christ, and the Holy Ghost, which beareth record of them, may be and abide in you forever. Amen." (Ether 12:41.)

Notes

1. *God's Greatest Gift* (Salt Lake City: Deseret Book Co., 1976), pp. 153, 155.

2. See "The Father and the Son: A Doctrinal Exposition by the First Presidency and the Twelve," 30 June 1916, in James E. Talmage, *Articles of Faith* (Salt Lake City: Deseret Book Co., 1972), pp. 465-73.

3. Bruce R. McConkie, "The Mystery of Godliness," *1985 Brigham Young University Devotional and Fireside Speeches* (Provo, Utah: Brigham Young University, 1985), p. 52.

4. See *Teachings of the Prophet Joseph Smith*, sel. Joseph Fielding Smith (Salt Lake City: Deseret Book Co., 1976), p. 328; Orson Pratt, "The Kingdom of God," in *Orson Pratt's Works* (Salt Lake City: Parker Pratt Robinson, 1965), pp. 46-48. See also Robert L. Millet and Joseph Fielding McConkie, *In His Holy Name* (Salt Lake City: Bookcraft, 1988), chapter 3.

5. See Bruce R. McConkie, *The Promised Messiah* (Salt Lake City: Deseret Book Co., 1978), pp. 360-61.

6. See "The Father and the Son," in Talmage, *Articles of Faith*, pp. 470-72.

7. McConkie, *The Promised Messiah*, p. 63; see also *A New Witness for the Articles of Faith* (Salt Lake City: Deseret Book Co., 1985), p. 69.

8. For confirmation that the Being on the mount was Jehovah and not Elohim, see James R. Clark, comp., *Messages of the First Presidency*, 6 vols. (Salt Lake City: Bookcraft, 1965-75), 4:269-71; McConkie, *The Promised Messiah*, p. 443.

9. Divine investiture of authority operates in circumstances other than those in which the Savior speaks on behalf of the Father. For example, the Holy Ghost speaks on behalf of Christ (Moses 5:9) and angels speak in behalf of the Lord (Revelation 22:8-13). It may well be that the words spoken to Nephi the night before the Savior was to be born (3 Nephi 1:13-14) were spoken by the Spirit or an angel in behalf of Christ. (See McConkie, *The Mortal Messiah* 1:349, note 1.)

10. *The Promised Messiah*, p. 371.

11. *The Mediation and Atonement of our Lord and Savior Jesus Christ* (Salt Lake City: Deseret News Co., 1982), p. 138.

12. *Teachings of the Prophet Joseph Smith*, p. 364.

13. *Teachings of the Prophet Joseph Smith*, p. 345.

14. See Bruce R. McConkie, "The Doctrinal Restoration," in *The Joseph Smith Translation: The Restoration of Plain and Precious Things*, ed. Monte S. Nyman and Robert L. Millet (Provo, Utah: Religious Studies Center, Brigham Young University, 1985), pp. 1-22.

*There is no flesh that can dwell in the
presence of God, save it be through the merits,
and mercy, and grace of the Holy Messiah.*
—2 Nephi 2:8

10

Relying Wholly upon His Merits

What mortal can snatch pride and selfishness, lust and lewdness from a natural man and create a clean heart in its place? Indeed, no man but the Man of Holiness and the Son of Man can do such things; these are works and wonders beyond the power of even the most spiritually mature Saints to do. Servants of the Lord can and do function at their Master's behest in administering the gospel to the children of men. Legal administrators—agents of the Lord—can and do represent their divine principal in leading lost souls back to the fold of the Good Shepherd. But the miracle of change, the miracle associated with the renovation and regeneration of fallen man, is the work of a God. The true Saints of God have come to know and rely upon that transcendent power.

Why Jesus Was the Savior

Lehi testified to his son Jacob that "redemption cometh in and through the Holy Messiah; for he is full of grace and truth." He continued: "Wherefore, how great the importance to make these things known unto the inhabitants of the earth, that they may know that there is no flesh that can dwell in the presence of God, save it be through the merits, and mercy, and grace of the Holy Messiah, who layeth down his life according to the flesh, and taketh it again by the power of the Spirit, that he may bring to pass the resurrection of the dead, being the first that should rise." (2 Nephi 2:6, 8.)

A number of significant doctrinal points surface in this poignant passage. First, we note with interest that Lehi's stress is not upon the importance of man's works or merits—as essential as they may be— but rather on the merits and mercy and grace of Christ. It is through what the Savior has done, the works and merits of the Lord Jesus that no mortal man could accomplish, that salvation is made available. As we have already noted, had there been no atonement there would be no salvation of any type or kind or nature. Earlier in Lehi's counsel to his son, the aged patriarch-prophet said: "Wherefore, thy soul shall be blessed, and thou shalt dwell safely with thy brother, Nephi; and thy days shall be spent in the service of thy God. Wherefore, I know that thou art redeemed, because of the righteousness of thy Redeemer; for thou hast beheld that in the fulness of time he cometh to bring salvation unto men." (2 Nephi 2:3.)

Second, the prophets are bold in declaring that we are able to rely on Christ because of his sinless state, because he qualified in every sense for salvation through his own merits, through his own moral perfection. He "was in all points tempted like as we are, yet without sin" (Hebrews 4:15). Christ never sinned, never took a wayward path. He never knew—until the hours of atonement—the awful agony of alienation from things holy; he never experienced until Gethsemane and Calvary the loss of the Spirit of the Father, the loss that follows in the wake of willful sin. Being perfect, therefore, he was qualified, capable, and more than willing to help us who are so very imperfect.

Further, and perhaps more important, Jesus of Nazareth was lit-erally the Son of the Almighty Elohim, and as such inherited from his exalted sire the powers of immortality, the ability to live forever. From his mother, the mortal Mary, he inherited mortality, the capacity to die. "Therefore doth my Father love me," Jesus stated, "because I lay down my life, that I might take it again. No man taketh it from me, but I lay it down of myself. I have power to lay it down, and I have power to take it again. This commandment have I received of my Father." (John 10:17-18.) Thus, in the language of Lehi, Christ laid down his life according to the flesh—he submitted to the universal commonality, death—and took it up again by the power of the Spirit: he rose from the tomb in glory by virtue of his inherited power over death. In describing the manner in which Jesus Christ was able to pay the "debt" incurred by man through the Fall and through individual sinfulness, C. S. Lewis has wisely observed:

> We are told that Christ was killed for us, that His death has washed out our sins, and that by dying he disabled death itself. That is the formula. That is Christianity. That is what has to be believed. Any theories we build up as to how Christ's death did all this are, in my view, quite secondary. . . . The [theory] most people have heard is the one . . . about our being let off because Christ had volunteered to bear a punishment instead of us. Now on the face of it that is a very silly theory. If God was prepared to let us off, why on earth did He not do so? And what possible point could there be in punishing an innocent person instead? None at all that I can see, if you are thinking of punishment in the police-court sense. On the other hand, if you think of a debt there is plenty of point in a person who has some assets paying it on behalf of someone who has not. Or if you take "paying the penalty," not in the sense of being punished, but in the more general sense of "standing the racket," or "footing the bill," then, of course, it is a matter of common experience that, when one person has got himself into a hole, the trouble of getting him out usually falls on a kind friend. . . .
>
> If I am drowning in a rapid river, a man who still has one foot on the bank may give me a hand which saves my life. Ought I to shout back (between my gasps) "No, it's not fair! You have an advantage! You're keeping one foot on the bank"? That advantage—call it "unfair" if you like—is the only reason why he can be of any use to me. To what will you look for help if you will not look to that which is stronger than yourself?[1]

Salvation Through His Merits Alone

It was in teaching the father of King Lamoni that Aaron, the son of Mosiah, "did expound unto him the scriptures from the creation of Adam, laying the fall of man before him, and their carnal state and also the plan of redemption, which was prepared from the foundation of the world, through Christ, for all whosoever would believe on his name. And since man had fallen he could not merit anything of himself; but the sufferings and death of Christ atone for their sins, through faith and repentance." (Alma 22:13-14.) Later in the Book of Mormon story we read that Anti-Nephi-Lehi, the brother of Lamoni and recent convert to the gospel path, prayed: "I . . . thank my God, that by opening this correspondence [that is, through the missionary labors of the sons of Mosiah] we have been convinced of our sins, and of the many murders which we have committed. And I also thank my God, yea, my great God, that he hath granted unto us that we might repent of these things, and also that he hath forgiven us of those our many sins and murders which we have committed, and taken away the guilt from our hearts, through the merits of his Son." (Alma 24:9-10.) In this regard, Bruce C. Hafen has stated:

> I once wondered if those who refuse to repent but who then satisfy the law of justice by paying for their own sins are then worthy to enter the celestial kingdom. The answer is no. The entrance requirements for celestial life are simply higher than merely satisfying the law of justice. For that reason, paying for our sins [our works] will not bear the same fruit as repenting of our sins [receiving the gift of grace offered through the Savior's atonement]. Justice is a law of balance and order and it must be satisfied, either through our payment or his. But if we decline the Savior's invitation to let him carry our sins, and then satisfy justice by ourselves, we will not yet have experienced the complete rehabilitation that can occur through a combination of divine assistance and genuine repentance. Working together, those forces have the power permanently to change our hearts and our lives.
> . . .
> The doctrines of mercy and repentance are rehabilitative, not retributive, in nature. The Savior asks for our repentance not merely to compensate him for paying our debt to justice, but also as a way of inducing us to undergo the process of development that will make our nature divine, giving us the capacity to live the celestial law. The "natural man" will remain an enemy to God forever—even after paying for his own sins—unless he also "becometh a saint through the atonement of Christ the Lord, and becometh as a child." (Mosiah 3:19.)
> As King Benjamin here suggests, the Atonement does more than pay for our sins. It is also the agent through which we develop a saintly nature.[2]

Conclusion

The prophet Moroni described those among the Nephites who had accepted the gospel and received the ordinances of salvation. Of them he said: "After they had been received unto baptism, and were wrought upon and cleansed by the power of the Holy Ghost, they were numbered among the people of the church of Christ; and their names were taken, that they might be remembered and nourished by the good word of God, to keep them in the right way, to keep them continually watchful unto prayer, relying alone upon the merits of Christ, who was the author and the finisher of their faith" (Moroni 6:4). The Saints in all ages receive with delight and overwhelming gratitude the words and works of Christ with unshaken faith in the Lord their Redeemer, "relying wholly upon the merits of him who is mighty to save" (2 Nephi 31:19).

Notes

1. *Mere Christianity* (New York: Macmillan, 1952), pp. 58-59, 61.
2. *The Broken Heart* (Salt Lake City: Deseret Book Co., 1989), pp. 7-8.

And in nothing doth man offend God,
or against none is his wrath kindled,
save those who confess not his hand in all things,
and obey not his commandments.
—D&C 59:21

11

Acknowledging His Hand
in All Things

*W*hen man focuses unduly upon himself and his own accomplishments he is unable to look to the source from whence his blessings spring; he is unable to focus on Christ the Lord. And thus "in nothing doth man offend God, or against none is his wrath kindled, save those who confess not his hand in all things, and obey not his commandments" (D&C 59:21).

Surely God's wrath is not kindled against the ungrateful because Deity in some way feels slighted, or because his feelings have been hurt, or because he needs our attention and our affections. God is an independent being and is possessed of all virtues and noble attributes in perfection. Insecurity is not characteristic of him who is Eternal. Nor is moodiness or pouting. His wrath is kindled against ungrateful man because such a one is worshiping a false god, and because allegiance to any object other than the true and living God is fruitless and unproductive: it cannot lead to life and salvation. When, however, men and women "thank the Lord [their] God in all things" (D&C 59:7), they are on a course that can lead them toward the realization of the measure of their creation and thus to happiness and fulfillment. Such persons—those who thank the Lord in all things, who acknowledge his hand in all things—are also those who acknowledge and gratefully accept and strive to keep his commandments. A vital part of accepting the gift of God is coming to see the hand of God in our lives.

Perceiving God's Involvement

Spiritual maturity means coming to see things "as they really are," and "as they really will be" (Jacob 4:13; compare D&C 93:24)—to see things as God sees them. The more a man or woman receives and cultivates the spirit of inspiration —the more nearly he or she gains "the mind of Christ" (1 Corinthians 2:16)—the more readily that person sees the workings of the Almighty in all phases of life. President George Q. Cannon thus observed:

> You take two persons, one who has the Spirit of God, whose mind is enlightened by that Spirit—the spirit of revelation, the same spirit that rested upon the prophets who wrote the revelations and prophecies we have—you take a man of that kind, and then take another who has none of that spirit, and put the two together, and the one man's eyes will be open to see the hand of God in all these events; he will notice his movements and his providence in everything connected with his work and they will be testimonies to him to strengthen his faith and furnish his mind with continual reasons for giving thanks to and worshipping God; while the man, who has not the spirit of God, will see nothing Godlike in the occurrences: nothing which he will view as supernatural. . . . his eyes will be closed, his heart will be hardened, and to all the evidences of the divinity of these things he will be impenetrable.[1]

President Joseph F. Smith also reminds us that the Almighty has "raised up philosophers among [men], teachers of men, to set the example, and to develop the mind and understanding of the human race in all nations of the world. God did it, but the world does not give credit to God, but gives it to men, to heathen philosophers. They give credit to them. I give it to God. And I tell you God knew the truth before they did, and through revelation they got it [Alma 29:8]. Let me say to you, my fellow workers in the cause of Zion, do not forget to acknowledge the hand of God in all things."[2] President Smith's son, Joseph Fielding Smith, taught over sixty years later:

We see a man with extraordinary gifts, or with great intelligence, and he is instrumental in developing some great principle. He and the world ascribe his great genius and wisdom to himself. He attributes his success to his own energies, labor, and mental capacity. He does not acknowledge the hand of the Lord in anything connected with his success, but ignores him altogether and takes the honor to himself. This will apply to almost all the world. In all the great modern discoveries in science, in the arts, in mechanics, and in all the material advancement of the age, the world says, "We have done it." The individual says, "I have done it," and he gives no honor or credit to the Lord.[3]

Not all of the doings, events, and consequences of life stem from God or may be traced to his Almighty hand. So much of the suffering and pain and agony of mortality is tied to man's inhumanity to man, or to the otherwise faulty use of agency. The First Presidency early in this century explained:

The agency of man is not interfered with by Divine Providence. . . . God, doubtless, could avert war, prevent crime, destroy poverty, chase away darkness, overcome error, and make all things bright, beautiful and joyful. But this would involve the destruction of a vital and fundamental attribute in man, the right of agency. It is for the benefit of His sons and daughters that they become acquainted with evil as well as good, with darkness as well as light, with error as well as truth, and with the results of the infraction of eternal laws. Therefore He has permitted the evils which have been brought about by the acts of His creatures, but will control their ultimate results for His own glory and the progress and exaltation of His sons and daughters when they have learned obedience by the things they suffer. . . . The foreknowledge of God does not imply His action in bringing about that which man does or refuses to do. The comprehension of this principle makes clear many questions that puzzle the uninformed as to the power and works of Deity.[4]

Trusting in His Mighty Arm

To acknowledge the Lord's hand is to acknowledge his omnipotence as well as the powerlessness and impotence of unillumined man. "O Lord," Nephi cried out in poignant soliloquy, "I have trusted in thee, and I will trust in thee forever. I will not put my trust in the arm of flesh; for I know that cursed is he that putteth his trust in the arm of flesh. Yea, cursed is he that putteth his trust in man or maketh flesh his arm." (2 Nephi 4:34; compare Jeremiah 17:5.) In fact, the fulness of the gospel was restored to the earth in our day in order to bring about that which the prophets had foretold: "The weak things of the world shall come forth and break down the mighty and strong ones, that man should not counsel his fellow man, neither trust in the arm of flesh—but that every man [armed with righteousness and clothed upon with the mantle of the Holy Spirit] might speak in the name of God the Lord, even the Savior of the world; that faith also might increase in the earth; that mine everlasting covenant might be established" (D&C 1:19-22). Those who fail to receive the gifts of grace proffered by God, who fail to acknowledge the divine in their lives, "seek not the Lord to establish his righteousness, but every man walketh in his own way, and after the image of his own god" (D&C 1:16). The early Saints were sorely chastened by the Lord, therefore, and told that they had "many things to do and to repent of; for behold, your sins have come up unto me, and are not pardoned, because you seek to counsel in your own ways" (D&C 56:14).

The Saints of the Most High come to acknowledge the hand of God when they forsake the flatteries and fineries of the world, devote themselves to their discipleship, and forfeit their own will to him who is both omniscient and all-loving. They become "prisoners of Christ" (Ephesians 3:1; Philemon 1:1)—they have waged a mighty warfare against the flesh and the powers of evil and have surrendered their all to the Lord of Hosts. "True discipleship," Elder Neal A. Maxwell has written, "is for volunteers only. Only volunteers will trust the Guide sufficiently to follow Him in the dangerous ascent which only He can lead." He continues:

> If instead of surrendering to Him we surrender to ourselves, we are surely bowing before an unjust and unwise emperor.
>
> There can be no conditions attached to unconditional surrender to God. Unconditional surrender means we cannot keep our obsessions, possessions, or cheering constituencies. Even our customized security blankets must go.
>
> Does this sound too severe and too sacrificing? If so, it is only until we realize that if we yield to Him, He will give us everything He has (D&C 84:38). Anyone, for example, who prepares to sit down at that culminating banquet with Jesus, Abraham, Isaac, and Jacob, cer-

tainly would not bring along his own beef jerky. Nor would he send an advance press agent to tout his accomplishments to that special company and in the presence of Him who trod the winepress alone (D&C 76:107).

Our personal trinkets, if carried even that far, are to be left outside at the doorstep or in the courtyard, where such clutter and debris would indicate the shedding of selfishness.

Some of us nevertheless feel as though we own ourselves, our time, our talents, and our possessions; these are signs of our self-sufficiency. Actually, God lends us breath and sustains us from moment to moment (Mosiah 2:21). Even our talents are gifts from Him. Whatever our possessions, these are merely on loan to us as accountable stewards. Possessions are not portable anyway. The submissive realize this.[5]

To acknowledge his hand is thus to admit that we are not our own; we are "bought with a price" (1 Corinthians 6:20). As one careful observer wisely pointed out, "The one principle of hell is: I am my own!"[6] True Saints, those with a hope in Christ, those who are pointed toward the highest heaven, know well that they are a peculiar—a *purchased*—people; they have been bought with the precious blood of the sinless Son of Man (1 Corinthians 6:19-20). Those who desire to be numbered among his flock gladly and gratefully acknowledge this.

Joseph Smith, the Prophet-Seer of this final dispensation, was and is a marvelous example of one whose will was swallowed up in the will of God. In writing to his beloved Emma, he remarked: "God is my friend. In him I shall find comfort. I have given my life into his hands. I am prepared to go at his call. I desire to be with Christ. I count not my life dear to me, only to do his will."[7]

Conclusion

To acknowledge the Lord's hand in all things is to admit and attest that the Lord Omniscient has a plan and a divine design for his children and a timetable for when things are to come to pass. To acknowledge the hand of God, therefore, is to be patient and persevering, to be flexible and faithful, knowing assuredly that "all things work together for good to them that love God" and trust in his purposes (Romans 8:28; compare D&C 90:24; 100:15). How true it is that "the more we become like Christ, the closer we will come to Him and the more we will trust Him. Submission, after all, is the ultimate adoration."[8]

Notes

1. In *Journal of Discourses* (Liverpool: F. D. Richards & Sons, 1855-86), 21:267.

2. *Young Woman's Journal*, June 1907, pp. 312-13.

3. In Conference Report, October 1969, p. 110.

4. *Deseret News*, 19 December 1914.

5. *"Not My Will, But Thine"* (Salt Lake City: Bookcraft, 1988), pp. 89, 92-93.

6. George MacDonald, *George MacDonald: An Anthology*, ed. C. S. Lewis (New York: Macmillan, 1978), p. 88.

7. Joseph Smith, *The Personal Writings of Joseph Smith*, ed. Dean C. Jessee (Salt Lake City: Deseret Book Co., 1984), p. 239, punctuation provided.

8. Neal A. Maxwell, *"Not My Will, But Thine,"* p. 127.

My grace is sufficient for thee;
for my strength is made perfect in weakness.
—*2 Corinthians 12:9*

12

From Weakness to Strength, from Grace to Grace

The fall of our first parents brought spiritual separation and alienation from things of holiness. But the infinite and eternal atonement opens the door to reunion with God through Christ. Because of our Lord's saving act, because of his perfect life and his unfathomable suffering, death, and rise to newness of life, all men and women are in a position to be reconciled to the Father. In speaking to God of the plight but the possibilities of mankind, Enoch stated: "Thou hast made me, and given unto me a right to thy throne, and not of myself, but through thine own grace" (Moses 7:59). Paul likewise pleaded with the Saints in his day: "Let us therefore come boldly unto the throne of grace, that we may obtain mercy, and find grace to help in time of need" (Hebrews 4:16). We may approach with boldness the holy throne of him who is Lord and God over all—approach with confidence or assurance that we will not be rejected—because of the mediation and intercession of Jesus the Christ, who has pleaded our cause and made everlasting salvation available.

God Grants Repentance

The return to the path of purity and peace through repentance is not simply a grand work that man must perform on his own. Once a person begins to exercise saving faith in Christ—knows of God and his attributes and knows that the course the person is now beginning to pursue is pleasing to the heavens—repentance will follow. That is to say, once a person knows the greatness and power and purity of him who is Lord, he also begins to sense the vast difference between himself and his God. But repentance is more than embarrassment. It is more than remorse. As we shall see shortly, repentance is a change of heart, a change of mind, a new direction, a new way of thinking and viewing the world. Such a course is both God-ordained and God-assisted; we cannot do it completely on our own. Repentance is granted and available as a free gift to man through the Atonement; through the grace and goodness of Jesus Christ, men and women are not only entitled to repent but also are enabled to do so.

In standing before the Sanhedrin, Peter and John bore a powerful witness of their Master. "We ought to obey God rather than men," Peter said fearlessly. "The God of our fathers raised up Jesus, whom ye slew and hanged on a tree. Him hath God exalted with his right hand to be a Prince and a Saviour, for to give repentance to Israel, and forgiveness of sins." (Acts 5:29-31; compare 11:18.) Paul likewise counseled Timothy: "Foolish and unlearned questions avoid, knowing that they do gender strifes. And the servant of the Lord must not strive; but be gentle unto all men, apt to teach, patient, in meekness instructing those that oppose themselves; if God peradventure will give them repentance to the acknowledging of the truth." (2 Timothy 2:23-25.)

Since God grants repentance, it cannot be viewed as a human work alone. Thus Amulek spoke of the meaning of the law of Moses and noted that "every whit" pointed to that great and last sacrifice of the Son of God, a sacrifice that would be both infinite and eternal. "And thus he shall bring salvation to all those who shall believe on his name; this being the intent of this last sacrifice, to bring about the bowels of mercy, which overpowereth justice, and bringeth about means unto men that they may have faith unto repentance." (Alma 34:14-15.)

C. S. Lewis has written in a thoughtful way about how God works in man to bring about repentance:

> Now repentance is no fun at all. It is something much harder than merely eating humble pie. It means unlearning all the self-conceit and self-will that we have been training ourselves into for thousands of

years. It means killing part of yourself, undergoing a kind of death. In fact, it needs a good man to repent. And here comes the catch. Only a bad person needs to repent: only a good person can repent perfectly. The worse you are the more you need it and the less you can do it. The only person who could do it perfectly would be a perfect person—and he would not need it.

Remember, this repentance, this willing submission to humiliation and a kind of death, is not something God demands of you before He will take you back and which He could let you off if He chose; it is simply a description of what going back to Him is like. If you ask God to take you back without it, you are really asking Him to let you go back without going back. It cannot happen. Very well, then, we must go through with it. But the same badness which makes us need it, makes us unable to do it. Can we do it if God helps us? Yes, but what do we mean when we talk of God helping us? We mean God putting into us a bit of Himself, so to speak. He lends us a little of His reasoning powers and that is how we think: He puts a little of His love into us and that is how we love one another. When you teach a child writing, you hold its hand while it forms the letters: that is, it forms the letters because you are forming them. We love and reason because God loves and reasons and holds our hand while we do it. Now if we had not fallen, that would be all plain sailing. But unfortunately we now need God's help in order to do something which God, in his own nature, never does at all—to surrender, to suffer, to submit, to die . . . But supposing God became a man—suppose our human nature which can suffer and die was amalgamated with God's nature in one person—then that person could help us. He could surrender His will, and suffer and die, because He was man; and He could do it perfectly because He was God.[1]

Indeed, the coming of the great Jehovah to earth to take a "tabernacle of clay"—what the Nephites called the "condescension of God"—and to lay down that tabernacle in his atoning sacrifice was the central event of all eternity, the consummate act of mercy and grace. As Abinadi declared, because Jesus of Nazareth was both God and man, spirit and flesh, Father and Son, he could subject himself to the flesh and at the same time accomplish the will of Elohim the Father (Mosiah 15:1-4). From Eden's dawn to the future millennial splendor, people on earth would look to the great Mediator of all men for direction and for deliverance from the paralyzing effects of sin. And because he would come, because he would live and suffer and die and rise again, repentance was granted and was freely available. Salvation would be free.

Overcoming Sinfulness

Conquering weakness involves more than merely detailing every sin and documenting every flaw of character. It surely consists of more than devoting a designated period of time to the mitigation of our more obvious personality hang-ups. Those who repent with all their hearts are renewed in their spirits and purified in their perspectives. They gain "the mind of Christ" (1 Corinthians 2:16) and come to view things as he does. The Greek word translated as repentance is *metanoia*, from *meta*, "after" and *noeo*, "to understand." To repent is literally to have an "afterthought," or to have a "change of mind." There is a related way to view these matters. *Meta* also means "above" or "beyond," as in the word *metaphysics*. To repent, in this sense, is to gain a perspective or view of things which is beyond the natural or carnal view; it is to see things from a different view, from a higher plane.

Overcoming our weakness consists of more than conquering individual weaknesses. Paul Tillich suggested that "in relation to God, it is not the particular sin as such that is forgiven but the act of separation from God and the resistance to reunion with him. It is sin which is forgiven in the forgiving of a particular sin."[2] Another Protestant theologian has suggested that "there is value in the practice sometimes followed by theologians whereby they distinguish between sin and sins. When the word is used generically in the singular it describes the condition of the person who is in bondage. A symptom of sin is that a person commits sins. In the eyes of the law or of the ethical theorist, the sins are freely chosen and a person is responsible for them. But theologically speaking, we need to look past the sins to the underlying sin, the sickness that needs to be cured, the bondage from which the sinner needs to be set free."[3]

Weakness to Strength Through Grace

Moroni feared that the future Gentiles would scoff at the simple plainness of his writings. But the Lord tenderly answered his concerns: "Fools mock, but they shall mourn; and my grace is sufficient for the meek, that they shall take no advantage of your weakness; and if men come unto me I will show unto them their weakness. I give unto men weakness that they may be humble; and my grace is sufficient for all men that humble themselves before me; for if they humble themselves before me, and have faith in me, then will I make weak things become strong unto them." (Ether 12:26-27; compare Jacob 4:7.)

Those who go to the Lord in earnest and pleading prayer—who have no thought of holding back, no desire to set the terms of the surrender of their will—will be granted a view of their weakness, of their fallen nature, and thus of their surpassing need for a Redeemer. Yes, of course they will come to sense individual sins and imperfections, but, more important, they will acknowledge before him whose is the all-searching eye that they are unworthy and unclean. They will desire to rid themselves and cleanse their hearts of sinfulness as well as of sins. These supplicants petition with a fervor known only to the hungry of soul: "O Jesus, thou Son of God, have mercy on me, who am in the gall of bitterness, and am encircled about by the everlasting chains of death" (Alma 36:18). They will plead with the Father: "O have mercy, and apply the atoning blood of Christ that we may receive forgiveness of our sins, and our hearts may be purified" (Mosiah 4:2). These are the poor in spirit—the bankrupt of soul—who come unto him (3 Nephi 12:3). They are filled.

In order to pull us from the lofty heights of self-assurance and overmuch self-reliance, God frequently provides weakness in the form of trials and trauma and difficulties and dilemmas. These plights of life force us to our knees and turn our hearts toward the divine Deliverer, the mighty Savior. Weakness not brought on by sin or foolishness, weakness, for example, in the form of physical or emotional difficulty; weakness in the form of setback or delay or family struggles or postponement of plans; weakness in the form of personal limitations—such circumstances can be turned by a loving and lifting Lord into strengths and blessings, given that the recipient of the challenge is patient and submissive and prayerful.

Some dark clouds have a silver lining; others simply bring thunderstorms; and the person who trusts in God will have his share of both. Behind some difficulties we will see the hand of the Lord, will envision the particular purpose for which we are called to suffer; behind others we will see few lessons for life but more of the same on the horizon. But the man or woman of God will have learned the patience of hope, even from the most devastating trials, declaring of God, as Job did: "Though he slay me, yet will I trust in him" (Job

13:15). The grace of him who suffered most but deserved least to suffer; the grace of him who came to give life and was put to death by those he came to save; the grace of him who, while he never displeased the Father, was left to tread the winepress alone, even the winepress of the fierceness of the wrath of Almighty God (D&C 76:107)—even he "can lift us from deep despair and cradle us midst any care."[4] In our moments of desperation and extremity, in our time of challenge and need, his grace is sufficient for us if we trust in him. The Lord's comforting assurance to the Apostle Paul has universal application: "My grace is sufficient for thee: for my strength is made perfect in weakness" (2 Corinthians 12:9).

From Grace to Grace

With divine assistance people are in a position to receive additional attributes and powers of the Spirit through repentance and subsequent faithfulness: they may receive what the scriptures speak of as "grace for grace." "May God grant, in his great fulness," Mormon pleaded, "that men might be brought unto repentance and good works, that they might be restored unto grace for grace, according to their works. And I would that all men might be saved." (Helaman 12:24-25.) To receive "grace for grace" is to receive of the Father as we give to others. In this, as in all other enterprises in this life, Jesus Christ is our exemplar and our pattern. Of him a modern revelation attests: "He received not of the fulness [of the glory of the Father] at the first, but received grace for grace" (D&C 93:12; compare John 1:16).

One Latter-day Saint writer has provided a description of the Savior's work as follows:

> Grace may be defined as an unearned gift or endowment given as a manifestation of divine love and compassion, for which the recipient does not pay an equivalent price. . . . When Jesus received the attributes and powers of His Father's glory, He received grace *for grace;* that is, He received the divine endowments of the Father's glory as He gave grace to others. Service and dedication to the welfare of others, in doing the will of the Father, therefore were keystone principles in Christ's spiritual development. Jesus had also covenanted with the Father that He would consecrate the glory which He would receive and develop in others to the Man of Holiness [Moses 4:2]. Here, too,

He promised to give grace in order to receive grace.[5]

The revelation cited above continues: "And [Christ] received not of the fulness at first, but continued from grace to grace, until he received a fulness" (D&C 93:13). To grow "from grace to grace" implies a developmental process, a progression from one level of spiritual attainment to a higher. Joseph Smith thus provided a definition of eternal life as that of knowing "the only wise and true God." He further taught: "You have got to learn how to be Gods yourselves, and to be kings and priests to God, the same as all Gods have done before you, namely, by going from one small degree to another, and from a small capacity to a great one; from grace to grace, from exaltation to exaltation, until you attain to the resurrection of the dead, and are able to dwell in everlasting burnings, and to sit in glory, as do those who sit enthroned in everlasting power."[6]

Conclusion

The revelation with which we began this doctrinal concept then establishes the meaning of worship: "I give unto you these sayings [concerning how Christ received grace for grace and grew from grace to grace] that you may understand and know how to worship, and know what you worship, that you may come unto the Father in my name, and in due time receive of his fulness. For if you keep my commandments you shall receive of his fulness, and be glorified in me as I am in the Father; therefore, I say unto you, you shall receive grace for grace." (D&C 93:19-20.) We worship God as did our Master, by serving our fellowmen and by growing line upon line to the point at which we are prepared and fit to dwell with the Father of lights.

> Perfect worship is emulation. We honor those whom we imitate. The most perfect way of worship is to be holy as Jehovah is holy. It is to be pure as Christ is pure. It is to do the things that enable us to become like the Father. The course is one of obedience, of living by every word that proceedeth forth from the mouth of God, of keeping the commandments.
> How do we worship the Lord? We do it by going from grace to grace, until we receive the fulness of the Father and are glorified in light and truth as is the case with our Pattern and Prototype, the Promised Messiah.[7]

Peter encouraged the disciples of Christ in his day to beware lest they be "led away with the error of the wicked" and thus "fall from your own steadfastness. But grow in grace, and in the knowledge of our Lord and Saviour Jesus Christ. To him be glory both now and forever. Amen." (2 Peter 3:17-18.)

Notes

1. *Mere Christianity* (New York: Macmillan, 1960), pp. 59-60.

2. *Systematic Theology*, 3 vols. (Chicago: University of Chicago Press, 1951-63), 3:225.

3. William Hordern, *Living by Grace* (Philadelphia: Westminster, 1975), pp. 93-94.

4. Neal A. Maxwell, *Notwithstanding My Weakness* (Salt Lake City: Deseret Book Co., 1981), p. 11.

5. Hyrum L. Andrus, *God, Man and the Universe* (Salt Lake City: Bookcraft, 1968), p. 206, italics in original.

6. *Teachings of the Prophet Joseph Smith*, sel. Joseph Fielding Smith (Salt Lake City: Deseret Book Co., 1976), pp. 346-47.

7. Bruce R. McConkie, *The Promised Messiah* (Salt Lake City: Deseret Book Co., 1978), pp. 568-69.

By the law no flesh is justified;
or, by the law men are cut off.
—2 Nephi 2:5

13

Justification by the Grace of Christ

*I*n a revelation given at the time of the organization of the restored Church, we find the following: "We know that all men must repent and believe on the name of Jesus Christ, and worship the Father in his name, and endure in faith on his name to the end, or they cannot be saved in the kingdom of God. And we know that justification through the grace of our Lord and Savior Jesus Christ is just and true." (D&C 20:29-30.) Justification is a legal term used in a scriptural context to describe one's relationship to God. To justify is to acquit, to vindicate, to pronounce righteous or innocent, free from sin.

Justification as an Act of Grace

Those who come with full purpose of heart to Christ through the gospel covenant receive the assurance that their Lord will renew them in spirit—he will justify them, will forgive their sins and thereby reconcile them with the Man of Holiness. This act of justification is an act of grace, made available by him who has the power so to do. We are not justified, strictly speaking, by our own labors, no matter how noble and righteous they may be. In fact, Paul taught, "Knowing that a man is not justified by the works of the law, but by the faith of Jesus Christ, even we have believed in Jesus Christ, that we might be justified by the faith of Christ, and not by the works of the law: for by the works of the law shall no flesh be justified" (Galatians 2:16; compare Romans 3:20; 2 Nephi 2:5). As man's part of the gospel covenant, he exercises faith in the Lord, receives the ordinances of salvation, and then agrees to live a life befitting his new fellowship with Christ.

Paul reminded the Roman Saints that "all have sinned and come short of the glory of God . . . being justified only by his grace through the redemption that is in Christ Jesus." Paul stated further, "Therefore we conclude that a man is justified by faith alone without the deeds of the law." (JST, Romans 3:23-24, 28.) In providing commentary upon these verses, Elder Bruce R. McConkie has written:

> Paul reasons and announces: All men have sinned; none, accordingly, are eligible to receive the glory of God, or in other words, to be saved. How, then, can sinners be saved? What will free them from their burden of sin and leave them clean and spotless? Or, as he expresses it, how can they be justified, meaning how can they be accounted and adjudged to be righteous?
>
> He has already shown there was no power in the law of Moses to do this, for those who had the law . . . were still in their sins. But, he proclaims, by the grace of God redemption from sin is available through Christ. Through his blood all men, Jew and Gentile alike, can gain a remission of their sins.
>
> What price must men pay for this precious gift? Not conformity to Mosaic standards, not compliance with the ordinances and performances of a dead law, but the price of faith, faith in the Lord Jesus Christ, faith that includes within itself enduring works of righteousness, which faith cannot so much as exist unless and until men conform their lives to gospel standards.
>
> Does salvation come, then, by works? No, not by the works of the law of Moses, and for that matter, not even by the more perfect works of the gospel itself. Salvation comes through Christ's atonement, through the ransom he paid, the propitiation he made; without this no good works on the part of men could redeem them from temporal death, which redemption is resurrection, or redeem them from spiritual death, which redemption is eternal life.[1]

Stated once again, men and women may be justified, pronounced clean and innocent, through the infinite gift of the atoning power of the Lord Jesus Christ. On their part, persons exercise faith in the

Redeemer, repent of their sins, are baptized by an authorized servant of God, receive and maintain the gift of the Holy Ghost, and do all in their power to remain thereafter true and faithful to the gospel covenant. "When we were yet without strength," Paul says, "Christ died for the ungodly. For scarcely for a righteous man will one die; yet peradventure for a good man some would even dare to die. But God commendeth his love toward us, in that, while we were yet sinners, Christ died for us. Much more then, being now justified by his blood, we shall be saved from wrath through him." (Romans 5:6-9.)

The Process of Justification

To be justified by God is to be made clean in spite of one's inability to repay the Master; to be made innocent in spite of one's lack of moral perfection. It is to be acquitted from sin through one's faith in Christ, faith that manifests itself in the works of righteousness (see Romans 2:6-7, 13; Galatians 5:6; Titus 3:8, 14). The Lord compensates for the chasm between man's strivings and God's perfection, between where a man really is (that is, in the case of one who is struggling with all his heart to comply with gospel law but falling short of the divine standard) and where he must eventually be (absolute moral perfection). But justification is both a journey and a destination, a process as well as a condition, and the heavens respond favorably (as we will discuss more directly in chapter 16) toward the righteous desires of the heart, as though those desires were actualized. Man's direction is as vital as his geography. "A comparison may be made," wrote Professor Sidney B. Sperry, "to a man on an escalator. We anticipate that he will reach a given floor if he stays on the escalator. So a person will eventually be justified, but may be regarded as being so now, if he retains a remission of sins (Mosiah 4:26) and continually shows his faith in God."[2]

As a vital part of the process of justification, God has made available the means by which one may not only *obtain* a remission of sins, but also *retain* that justified state from day to day. King Benjamin thus spoke: "And now, for the sake . . . of retaining a remission of your sins from day to day, that ye may walk guiltless before God," he testified, "I would that ye should impart of your substance to the poor, every man according to that which he hath, such as feeding the hungry, clothing the naked, visiting the sick and administering to their relief, both spiritually and temporally, according to their wants" (Mosiah 4:26). In the same vein, Mormon described the Nephite Christian community as those who, in contrast to the people who were proud and high-minded, "were abasing themselves, succoring those who stood in need of their succor, such as imparting their substance to the poor and the needy, feeding the hungry, and suffering all manner of afflictions, for Christ's sake, who should come according to the spirit of prophecy; looking forward to that day, thus retaining a remission of their sins" (Alma 4:13-14).

We exercise appropriate faith in our Master by involving ourselves in the work of the Master—the work of searching out and caring for the needy; the Savior's most significant blessings come in the form of justifying us and cleansing us from sin. Though a person may not be perfect in all respects, his attitudes and deeds toward his fellowmen evidence his devotion to the Lord and his desire to be in harmony with the divine will. The brother of our Lord attested that "he which converteth the sinner from the error of his way shall save a soul from death, and shall hide a multitude of sins" (James 5:20), not only the sins of the wayward, but also his own. Joseph Smith the Prophet thus explained that "to be justified before God we must love one another: we must overcome evil; we must visit the fatherless and the widow in their affliction, and we must keep ourselves unspotted from the sins of the world: for [and now notice that such Christian service and saintly attributes evidence one's faith] such virtues flow from the great fountain of pure religion, strengthening our faith by adding every good quality that adorns the children of the blessed Jesus."[3]

Justification Through the Holy Spirit of Promise

After a person has received the ordinances of salvation; after he has made covenant with Christ to follow him and keep his commandments; and when he progresses to the point at which God's ways are his ways, where Christ's mind is his mind, where he hungers and thirsts after righteousness and lives by every word of God—when he reaches that point, that person will receive the justifying seal of the Holy Ghost, the ratifying approval of that Holy Spirit of Promise that grants one consummate peace here and promises everlasting salvation with God and angels hereafter. The Saints of our day have been charged to "learn that he who doeth the works of righteousness shall receive his reward, even peace in this world, and eternal life in the world to come" (D&C 59:23).

After having been taught of the necessity for the new birth, of being reborn through water and blood and spirit, Adam was further instructed by the Lord: "For by the water ye keep the commandment; by the Spirit ye are justified, and by the blood ye are sanctified" (Moses 6:60). Elder Bruce R. McConkie has written: "The law of justification is simply this: 'All covenants, contracts, bonds, obligations, oaths, vows, performances, connections, associations, or expectations' (D&C 132:7), in which men must abide to be saved and exalted, must be entered into and performed in righteousness so that the Holy Spirit can justify the candidate for salvation in what has been done. (1 Ne. 16:2; Jac. 2:13-14; Alma 41:15; D&C 98; 132:1, 62.) *An act that is justified by the Spirit is one that is sealed by the Holy Spirit of Promise, or in other words, ratified and approved by the Holy Ghost.*"[4] Our revelations thus speak of the candidates for celestial glory as those who "overcome by faith, and are sealed by the Holy Spirit of promise, which the Father sheds forth upon all those who are just and true." Such persons are "just men made perfect through Jesus the mediator of the new covenant, who wrought out this perfect atonement through the shedding of his own blood." (D&C 76:53, 69; compare 129:3; 138:12.)

Justification and Faith in Christ

In an excellent discussion of the law of justification, Gerald N. Lund has written:

> In the scriptural sense of the term, it is impossible for a man to be justified (brought back into a proper relationship with God) by his own works, because no one can keep the law perfectly. This was the very mistake that the Pharisees fell into with regard to the Mosaic law. We sometimes smile at their tremendously careful attempts to define the law and what was acceptable to it; but if you hold that a man is brought into the proper relationship with God by his own works alone, then theirs was a logical position to take. If the tiniest infraction of the law puts one's relationship to God in jeopardy, then one must be extremely careful about any violation. The early rabbis simply carried that idea to its extreme. . . .
>
> Paul said we are justified *through* and *by* faith (see Gal. 2:16; Rom.

3:28), which is the first principle of the gospel. In other words, faith is the principle that activates the power of the Atonement in our lives, and we are put back into a proper relationship with God (justification) as faith activates that power. There are marvelous implications in this concept. . . .

We are like a powerhouse on a mighty river. The powerhouse has no power residing in itself; the potential power rests in the energy of the river. When that source of power flows through the generators of the power plant, power is transferred from the river to the power plant and sent out into the homes (lives) of others. So it is with faith. The power to achieve justification does not reside in man. Man requires the power of the atonement of Christ flowing into him. If no power is being generated, one does not—indeed, cannot—turn the generators by hand (justification by works); but rather, an effort is made to remove those things which have blocked the power from flowing into the generators (working righteousness as a result of faith). With this background then, one can understand why the scriptures clearly stress that faith includes works (see James 2:17-26); that is, obedience, commitment, and repentance—these are the works of faith that open up the channels so that the power of the atoning sacrifice of Christ can flow into us, redeem us from sin, and bring us back into the presence of God. Disobedience and wickedness damn those channels. (How literal is the word *damnation!*) The righteous works in themselves do not save us. The atoning power of God saves us. But our righteous works, activated by our faith in the Savior, are the condition for the operation of that power. Thus, each of us has something to say about whether he will be able to seek the gift and power of the Atonement in his behalf.[5]

Conclusion

Paul expressed beautifully the relationship between the grace of God manifest to us through justification from sin, and how our faith in Christ—which leads to righteous works—may be activated. He spoke to Titus of the love of God shown by our Savior, "not by works of righteousness which we have done, but according to his mercy he saved us, by the washing of regeneration, and renewing of the Holy Ghost; which he shed on us abundantly through Jesus Christ our Saviour; that being justified by his grace, we should be made heirs according to the hope of eternal life. This is a faithful saying, and these things I will that thou affirm constantly, that they which have believed in God might be careful to maintain good works. These things are good and profitable unto men." (Titus 3:4-8.)

Notes

1. *Doctrinal New Testament Commentary*, 3 vols. (Salt Lake City: Bookcraft, 1965-73), 2:230-31.

2. *Paul's Life and Letters* (Salt Lake City: Bookcraft, 1955), p. 176.

3. *Teachings of the Prophet Joseph Smith*, sel. Joseph Fielding Smith (Salt Lake City: Deseret Book Co., 1976), p. 76.

4. *Mormon Doctrine*, 2d ed. (Salt Lake City: Bookcraft, 1966), p. 408, italics in original.

5. "Salvation: By Grace or by Works?" *Ensign*, April 1981, pp. 20-21, 22-23, italics in original.

14

Sanctification by the Grace of Christ

$\mathcal{W}$e glory in the saving grace of our Lord Jesus Christ, "who hath abolished death, and hath brought life and immortality to light through the gospel" (2 Timothy 1:10). The gospel is indeed the good news, the glad tidings, "that he came into the world, even Jesus, to be crucified for the world, and to bear the sins of the world, and *to sanctify the world, and to cleanse it from all unrighteousness*" (D&C 76:41, italics added). Christ came to make saints of sinners, to open the way to holiness, to reconcile mankind to the Father, and lead back to the eternal presence all who will be led. Jesus the Christ seeks to make of those who receive him a kingdom of priests and priestesses, a holy nation. "Be ye holy," he has commanded, "for I am holy" (1 Peter 1:16; see also Leviticus 11:44; Exodus 19:5-6).

Sanctified Through His Blood

We know "that sanctification through the grace of our Lord and Savior Jesus Christ is just and true" (D&C 20:31). Jesus Christ is the means by which men and women are sanctified, made holy and clean, and his is the only name through which fallen creatures may be renewed and renovated and lifted spiritually to that plane which characterizes him who is the embodiment of holiness. Moroni explained that ultimately, if we deny not the power of God, we may be "sanctified in Christ by the grace of God, through the shedding of the blood of Christ, which is in the covenant of the Father unto the remission of [our] sins, that [we] become holy, without spot" (Moroni 10:33).

Jesus was and is the light and life of the world, and "the life of the flesh is in the blood . . . for it is the blood that maketh an atonement for the soul" (Leviticus 17:11). Thus it is that the Lord explained to Adam: "By the water ye keep the commandment [the commandment to be baptized]; by the Spirit [the cleansing agent, the Holy Ghost] ye are justified, and by the blood [the "precious blood of Christ, as of a lamb without blemish and without spot" (1 Peter 1:19)] ye are sanctified" (Moses 6:60). The scriptural record says of the great prophet Enoch: "Enoch looked; and from Noah, he beheld all the families of the earth; and he cried unto the Lord, saying: When shall the day of the Lord come? When shall the blood of the Righteous be shed, that all that mourn may be sanctified and have eternal life?" The Lord God responded: "It shall be in the meridian of time, in the days of wickedness and vengeance." (Moses 7:45-46.) Truly, as the resurrected Savior stated to his American Hebrews, "no unclean thing can enter into [God's] kingdom; therefore nothing entereth into his rest save it be those who have washed their garments in my blood, because of their faith, and the repentance of all their sins, and their faithfulness unto the end" (3 Nephi 27:19).

Sanctified by the Spirit

To be *justified* is to be pronounced clean, to be decreed innocent, to be delivered and protected from the demands of God's justice, to be free from sin. This comes as one exercises faith in Christ and enters into a covenant relationship with him who is the Mediator of the new covenant. But the actual cleansing, the literal purification, does not take place through water baptism alone. Rather, one must receive the baptism of fire and the Holy Ghost in order to begin the process of sanctification. Nephi explained: "Wherefore, do the things which I have told you I have seen that your Lord and your Redeemer should do; for, for this cause have they been shown unto me, that ye might know the gate by which ye should enter. For the gate by which ye should enter is repentance and baptism by water; and then cometh a remission of your sins by fire and by the Holy Ghost" (2 Nephi 31:17; compare 3 Nephi 12:2).

Moroni observed, in speaking of those who came into the true Church, that "after they had been received unto baptism, and were wrought upon and cleansed by the power of the Holy Ghost, they were numbered among the people of the church of Christ" (Moroni 6:4). "Sins are remitted," Elder Bruce R. McConkie has written, "not in the waters of baptism, as we say in speaking figuratively, but when we receive the Holy Ghost. It is the Holy Spirit of God that erases carnality and brings us into a state of righteousness. We become clean when we actually receive the fellowship and companionship of the Holy Ghost. It is then that sin and dross and evil are burned out of our souls as though by fire. The baptism of the Holy Ghost is the baptism of fire."[1]

Likewise Elder Orson Pratt explained that "the baptism of the Holy Ghost cannot be dispensed with by the believer, any more than the baptism of water. To be born of the water, only justifies the sinner of past sins; but to be born, afterwards, of the Holy Ghost, sanctifies him and prepares him for spiritual blessings in this life, and for eternal life in the world to come."[2] Though the scriptures affirm repeatedly that it is by the purifying blood of the Messiah that men are sanctified and made pure, holy writ also attests that the medium through which this sanctification is accomplished is the Holy Ghost. Alma, in speaking to the Nephite people of the Church, proposed a series of questions that might serve as a type of spiritual checklist. One of those questions was: "Will ye persist in supposing that ye are better one than another; yea, will ye persist in the persecution of your brethren, who humble themselves and do walk after the holy order of God, wherewith they have been brought into this church, having been sanctified by the Holy Spirit, and they do bring forth works which are meet for repentance—yea, and will you persist in turning your backs upon the poor, and the needy, and in withholding your substance from them?" (Alma 5:54-55.) Christ taught the Nephites that "this is the commandment: Repent, all ye ends of the earth, and come unto me and be baptized in my name, that ye may be sanctified by the reception of the Holy Ghost, that ye may stand spotless before me at the last day" (3 Nephi 27:20; compare D&C 84:33).

"Strictly speaking, men are sanctified by the Spirit, and they are justified by the Spirit; but in a larger sense, they are sanctified by the blood, and they are justified by the blood, because the blood of Christ (meaning his atonement, wherein he shed his blood) is the foundation upon which all things rest. Thus, by way of accurate exposition, we are justified by the Spirit because of the blood of Christ."[3]

Free from the Effects of Sin

To be justified is to be free from sin, to be legally right before God. To be sanctified is to be free from the *effects* of sin, to have had sinfulness and the enticements of sin rooted out of our hearts and desires. To be sanctified in regard to vice is to shudder and shake at its appearance, to feel a revulsion for whatever allurements would detour or detain the human heart. It is to be as Jacob was: "Behold," he said, "my soul abhorreth sin, and my heart delighteth in righteousness" (2 Nephi 9:49; compare 4:31; Jacob 2:5). It is to be like the ancient people of God described by Alma: "They were called after this holy order, and were sanctified, and their garments were washed white through the blood of the Lamb. Now they, after being sanctified by the Holy Ghost, having their garments made white, being pure and spotless before God, could not look upon sin save it were with abhorrence; and there were many, exceedingly great many, who were made pure and entered into the rest of the Lord their God." (Alma 13:11-12.)

Orson Pratt has provided an insightful look into the nature of being sanctified by the Spirit through the blood of Christ:

> Water Baptism is only a preparatory cleansing of the believing penitent; it is only a condition of a cleansing from sin; whereas, the Baptism of fire and the Holy Ghost cleanses more thoroughly, by renewing the inner man, and by purifying the affections, desires, and thoughts which have long been habituated in the impure ways of sin.
>
> Without the aid of the Holy Ghost, a person . . . would have but very little power to change his mind, at once, from its habituated course, and to walk in newness of life. Though his sins may have been cleansed away, yet so great is the force of habit, that he would, without being renewed by the Holy Ghost, be easily overcome, and contaminated again by sin. Hence, it is infinitely important that the affections and desires should be, in a measure, changed and renewed, so as to cause him to hate that which he before loved, and to love that which

he before hated: to thus renew the mind of man is the work of the Holy Ghost.[4]

This change of nature, change of personality, change of desires and passions, is accomplished through the purging powers of the Holy Ghost. But it is accomplishable because of the atoning blood of Jesus Christ. A modern prophet, President Ezra Taft Benson, has reminded us: "The Lord works from the inside out. The world works from the outside in. The world would take people out of the slums. Christ takes the slums out of people, and then they take themselves out of the slums. The world would mold men by changing their environment. Christ changes men, who then change their environment. The world would shape human behavior, but Christ can change human nature. . . . Yes, Christ changes men, and changed men can change the world. Men changed by Christ will be captained by Christ. . . . Finally, men captained by Christ will be consumed in Christ."[5]

Let the Sanctified Take Heed

In a revelation given at the time of the organization of the latter-day Church, the Saints learned: "There is a possibility that man may fall from grace and depart from the living God; therefore let the church take heed and pray always, lest they fall into temptation; yea, and even let those who are sanctified take heed also" (D&C 20:32-34). Though one has gotten onto that strait and narrow path that leads to life; though one has navigated that path and partaken of the fruits of the atonement of Jesus Christ and known the consummate joys of acceptance into the fold and fellowship with the Saints; though one has risen to levels of spiritual grace wherein he has partaken of the fruits and blessings of the Spirit—despite these experiences, there is a critical need for one to be "steadfast and immovable, always abounding in good works" (Mosiah 5:15), enduring faithfully to the end of one's mortal days. Even those members of the Church who have enjoyed the sanctifying and cleansing blessings of the Spirit need to guard their attitudes and their actions, to watch and pray continually, lest they "fall from grace."

In one sense, Saints of the Most High fall from grace whenever they commit sin, for in so doing they separate themselves temporarily from the Spirit of God and rob themselves of that direction and comfort available through sustained righteousness. No man or woman will achieve the ultimate, the ideal of perfection in this life, though the Saints are under covenant to strive for that goal. Thus the process of justification, made possible through the ransoming and mediating power of our Lord and Savior—available to us as Latter-day Saints as we involve ourselves in Christian service and deeds of faith and righteousness—allows us the privilege of turning regularly to him who is mighty to save and of thus retaining a remission of sins from day to day.

There is also a scriptural sense in which those who have made sure their calling and election to eternal life—have received the assurance and promise of exaltation—are designated as the sanctified. "There has been a day of calling," a revelation declared, "but the time has come for a day of choosing; and let those be chosen that are worthy. And it shall be manifest unto my servant, by the voice of the Spirit, those that are chosen; and they shall be sanctified." (D&C 105:35-36.) In offering an insightful commentary upon these verses, Elder McConkie has written: "Many are called to the Lord's work, but few are chosen for eternal life. So that those who are chosen may be sealed up unto eternal life, the scripture says [cites D&C 105:36]. They are chosen by the Lord, but the announcement of their calling and election is delivered by the Spirit."[6] Should a person forsake the faith and fall prey to the spirit of bitter apostasy after having risen to this supernal level—something highly unusual, inasmuch as one's disposition toward willful sin decreases with continued faithfulness—then such a person would definitely have "fallen from grace."

"It is impossible," Paul wrote, "for those who were once enlightened, and have tasted of the heavenly gift, and were made partakers of the Holy Ghost, and have tasted the good word of God, and the powers of the world to come, if they shall fall away, to renew them again unto repentance; seeing they crucify to themselves the Son of God afresh, and put him to an open shame." Paul described such a person as one who had "trodden under foot the Son of God," a person who had "counted the blood of the covenant, wherewith he was sanctified, an unholy thing, and hath done despite unto the Spirit of grace." (Hebrews 6:4-6; 10:29.) The Prophet Joseph Smith explained:

There is a superior intelligence bestowed upon such as obey the Gospel with full purpose of heart, which, if sinned against, the apostate is left naked and destitute of the Spirit of God, and he is, in truth, nigh unto cursing, and his end is to be burned. When once that light which was in them is taken from them, they become as much darkened as they were previously enlightened, and then, no marvel, if all their power should be enlisted against the truth, and they, Judas like, seek the destruction of those who were their greatest benefactors. What nearer friend on earth, or in heaven, had Judas than the Savior? And his first object was to destroy Him.[7]

In Joseph Smith's day a theological debate raged between those who believed in the predestination of souls—and thus that men and women were called and chosen, elected to salvation from the foundation of the world and thus could not "fall from grace"—and those who believed that man had a major role in the salvation process and therefore could periodically fall from that level of divine acceptance. Only three months before his death, the Prophet made the following remarks concerning this doctrinal controversy:

The doctrine that the Presbyterians and Methodists have quarreled so much about—once in grace, always in grace [the Presbyterians], or falling away from grace [the Methodists], I will say a word about. They are both wrong. Truth takes a road between them both, for while the Presbyterian says: "Once in grace, you cannot fall"; the Methodist says: "You can have grace today, fall from it tomorrow, next day have grace again; and so follow on, changing continually." But the doctrine of the Scriptures and the spirit of Elijah would show them both false, and take a road between them both; for, according to the Scripture, if men have received the good word of God, and tasted of the powers of the world to come, if they shall fall away, it is impossible to renew them again, seeing they have crucified the Son of God afresh, and put Him to an open shame; so there is a possibility of falling away; you could not be renewed again, and the power of Elijah cannot seal against this sin [the unpardonable sin, the sin against the Holy Ghost], for this is a reserve made in the seals and power of the Priesthood.[8]

In short, it is true that men and women may fall from grace periodically as they climb the path to celestial life. There is, however, a level of transcendent grace—a height toward which the Saints aspire and press with patient maturity and steadfastness—a summit which, when once scaled, necessitates that one show even greater vigilance and readiness against the onslaughts of the destroyer. Indeed, the price to be paid—no matter what the level of our spiritual attainments—is to remain faithful and true to our covenants and our commitments to the end of our days. If we leave this life firm in the faith, in good standing and in full fellowship, we will not "fall from grace" in the world of spirits or any time thereafter. Rather, we will continue in that same direction, with perhaps even greater intensity, among persons of like disposition and will go on to the highest and greatest of eternal rewards. "And if you keep my commandments and endure to the end," the Lord has reminded us in this day, "you shall have eternal life, which gift is the greatest of all the gifts of God" (D&C 14:7).

Conclusion

Sanctification is a condition. And sanctification is a process. It comes in time to those who yield their hearts to God (Helaman 3:35), to those whose minds are single to God and his glory (D&C 88:67-68), to those who trust in and seek after the redeeming grace of him who calls his people to the way of holiness. "Those who go to the celestial kingdom of heaven," Elder McConkie explained to Brigham Young University students, "have to be sanctified, meaning that they become clean and pure and spotless. They've had evil and sin and iniquity burned out of their souls as though by fire. . . . It is a process. Nobody is sanctified in an instant, suddenly. But if we keep the commandments and press forward with steadfastness after baptism, then degree by degree and step by step we sanctify our souls until that glorious day when we're qualified to go where God and angels are."9

Notes

1. *A New Witness for the Articles of Faith* (Salt Lake City: Deseret Book Co., 1985), p. 290; see also p. 239; *Teachings of the Prophet Joseph Smith*, comp. Joseph Fielding Smith (Salt Lake City: Deseret Book Co., 1976), p. 314.

2. From N. B. Lundwall, comp., *A Compilation Containing the*

Lectures on Faith . . . Also a Treatise on True Faith by Orson Pratt. . . . (Salt Lake City: Bookcraft, n. d.), p. 88.

3. Bruce R. McConkie, *Doctrinal New Testament Commentary,* 3 vols. (Salt Lake City: Bookcraft, 1965-73), 2:239.

4. *The Holy Spirit* [pamphlet] (Liverpool, 1852), pp. 56-57.

5. In Conference Report, October 1985, pp. 5-6.

6. *A New Witness for the Articles of Faith* (Salt Lake City: Deseret Book Co., 1985), p. 270.

7. *Teachings of the Prophet Joseph Smith,* sel. Joseph Fielding Smith (Salt Lake City: Deseret Book Co., 1976), p. 67.

8. *Teachings of the Prophet Joseph Smith,* pp. 338-39.

9. "Jesus Christ and Him Crucified," *1976 Devotional Speeches of the Year* (Provo, Utah: Brigham Young University Press, 1977), p. 399.

After ye are reconciled unto God, . . .
it is only in and through the grace of God
that ye are saved.
—2 Nephi 10:24

15

Grace and Works:
The Essential Balance

*C*onfusion and uncertainty continue to exist in the minds of people throughout the world concerning the Latter-day Saints' view of Jesus Christ and the work of redemption. Much of this confusion is no doubt reflected in the conclusion by some that the Latter-day Saints are not Christian. Though it is difficult to fathom how people who are at least vaguely familiar with the Book of Mormon could draw such conclusions, accusations and innuendoes persist.

By Grace or by Works?

A typical description of the Latter-day Saint view of Christ and the Atonement is contained in the following paragraph written some years ago by the religion editor of a prominent national magazine:

> In Mormon scriptures, the story of Adam and Eve is accepted as literal truth. . . . According to Mormon tradition, not only did Adam's fall make procreation possible, it also established the conditions for human freedom and moral choice. Unlike orthodox Christians, *Mormons believe that men are born free of sin and earn their way to godhood by the proper exercise of free will, rather than through the grace of Jesus Christ. Thus Jesus' suffering and death in the Mormon view were brotherly acts of compassion, but they do not atone for the sins of others.* For this

reason, Mormons do not include the cross in their iconography nor do they place much emphasis on Easter.[1]

It is frustrating and terribly unfortunate that we as a church should be so misrepresented. It is sad that persons should fail to see in our lives as well as our literature that Jesus Christ is the focus of our faith and his atonement the fundamental principle of our religion.[2] Such attitudes—that Mormons are not Christian or that we do not believe in salvation by the grace of Christ—may be due in large part to our tendency to react (and perhaps overreact) to what we perceive to be an overreliance by Protestant Christianity upon salvation by grace alone.

Before leaving on a mission, for example, I approached one of my priesthood leaders with the question, "What does it mean to be saved by grace?" Having been raised in the Southern States and in the "Bible Belt," I had heard the phrase many times from my non-LDS friends.

My priesthood leader—a powerful preacher of the gospel and one who knew the doctrines well—responded quickly: "We don't believe in that."

I asked further: "We don't believe in salvation by grace? Why not?"

His comeback: "Because the Baptists do!"

Without question, the doctrinal restoration for which Joseph Smith was the human instrument was essential in tearing away the theological cobwebs of centuries, pulling back the veil, and revealing God anew; in restoring plain and precious truths that had been lost from the Bible; and in providing doctrinal texts and contexts, a proper setting and background for understanding all other aspects of life. We need not, however, swing to extremes unnecessarily. The Baptists also believe in baptism by immersion. The Roman Catholics believe that priesthood authority is necessary for salvation. The Jews (at least anciently) believed the temple to be the central focus of community worship. We need not deny or flee from any of these doctrinal postures merely because others accept them; truth is to be found in varying degrees in many forums. Although the Lord has restored to us the fulness of the gospel, we should not be surprised to find meaningful truths elsewhere in the religious world.

Some time after the article mentioned above had appeared, one person responded negatively in writing, deeply concerned that the writer could have "spent as much time as he did among the Mormons" only to come away with a skewed perception of Latter-day Saint theology. The religion editor answered the concern as follows: "I did read several books of Mormon scripture and theology before writing the article. My intent, however, was *not* to review books but rather to report how representative members of the LDS Church describe and interpret their own traditions. . . . The point is to determine what doctrines of a church are genuinely infused into the lifeblood of its adherents."[3]

The problem may well arise from more than bias on the part of an uninformed or hostile press, more than bigotry on the part of ministers who feel threatened by the growing Latter-day Saint presence in the religious world. It just may be that as Church members we talk of Christ too seldom, rejoice in Christ too seldom, preach of Christ too seldom, and that as a result not only our children but also many friends and bystanders do not know to what source we look for a remission of our sins (see 2 Nephi 25:26). It may be that too many are confused as to exactly where we stand on the vital issue of salvation. As this work has sought to demonstrate, the scriptures and the prophets are bold in testifying of the proper relationship—the essential balance—between the merits of Christ and the merits of man.

The Apostle Paul and Martin Luther

To begin with, let us consider the types of extremes to which people gravitate in regard to grace and works. The Apostle Paul encountered at least two groups of people who needed to rely upon the works and mercies and atoning grace of Jesus Christ and rely much less upon their own labors and achievements. Envisioning that situation, Elder Bruce R. McConkie explained:

> On the one hand, we are preaching to Jews who, in their lost and fallen state, have rejected their Messiah and who believe they are saved by the works and performances of the Mosaic law.
> On the other hand, we are preaching to pagans—Romans, Greeks, those in every nation—who know nothing whatever about the Messianic word, or of the need for a Redeemer, or of the working out of the infinite and eternal atonement. They worship idols, the forces of nature, the heavenly bodies, or whatever suits their fancy. As with the

Jews, they assume that this or that sacrifice or appeasing act will please the Deity of their choice and some vague and unspecified blessings will result.

Can either the Jews or the pagans be left to assume that the works they do will save them? Or must they forget their little groveling acts of petty worship, gain faith in Christ, and rely on the cleansing power of his blood for salvation?

They must be taught faith in the Lord Jesus Christ and to forsake their traditions and performances. Surely we must tell them they cannot be saved by the works they are doing, for man cannot save himself. Instead they must turn to Christ and rely on his merits and mercy and grace.[4]

We thus find Paul writing, for example, to the Ephesian Saints as follows: "By grace are ye saved through faith; and that not of yourselves: it is the gift of God: not of works, lest any man should boast" (Ephesians 2:8-9).

Some fifteen centuries later Martin Luther came face to face with a mother church caught up in a system of works-righteousness as well as in an ever-growing emphasis upon the payment of indulgences. Luther struggled both with his allegiance to the church and with his own soul—ever questioning his worth and berating himself because of the pull of the flesh. In Luther's own words:

> I greatly longed to understand Paul's Epistle to the Romans and nothing stood in the way but that one expression, "the justice of God," because I took it to mean that justice whereby God is just and deals justly and punishes the unjust.
>
> My situation was that, although an impeccable monk, I stood before God as a sinner troubled in conscience, and I had no confidence that my merit would assuage him. Therefore I did not love a just and angry God, but rather hated and murmured against him. Yet I clung to the dear Paul and had a great yearning to know what he meant.
>
> Night and day I pondered until I saw the connection between the justice of God and the statement that "the just shall live by his faith." Then I grasped that the justice of God is that righteousness by which through grace and sheer mercy God justifies us through faith. Thereupon I felt myself to be reborn and to have gone through open doors into paradise. The whole of scripture took on a new meaning, and whereas before the "justice of God" had filled me with hate, now it became to me inexpressibly sweet in greater love. The passage of Paul became to me a gate to heaven.[5]

Luther's rebellion against Roman Catholicism and the mandatory works stipulated by that church led him into reformation, a call for the cleansing of what he perceived to be a polluted vessel. It also led him to formulate and espouse the doctrine of salvation *by grace alone* through faith alone. Millions of Protestants worldwide have come to view salvation as that which was purchased by Christ and which requires little more than confession and acceptance of Jesus as Savior.

Cheap or Costly Grace?

We are confronted today by an army of religionists who proclaim that salvation was wrought on a cross some two thousand years ago; that there is absolutely nothing that any person can do today that will impact upon his or her personal salvation other than offer a verbal profession of the Lord Jesus, a pledge of allegiance for Christ. Crusades and revivals almost without number dot the planet, nearly all of which conclude with an invitation by the evangelist to come forward, accept and receive Jesus into the heart, and acknowledge thereafter that on that occasion salvation was realized. Unfortunately, such a view of salvation has produced in hosts of otherwise earnest persons a false sense of spiritual security, has resulted in their creation of what the German theologian Dietrich Bonhoeffer called "cheap grace."

> Cheap grace means grace sold on the market like cheapjack's wares. The sacraments, the forgiveness of sin, and the consolations of religion are thrown away at cut prices. Grace is represented as the Church's inexhaustible treasury, from which she showers blessings with generous hands, without asking questions or fixing limits. Grace without price; grace without cost! The essence of grace, we suppose, is that the account has been paid in advance; and, because it has been paid, everything can be had for nothing. Since the cost was infinite, the possibilities of using and spending it are infinite. What would grace be if it were not cheap? . . .
>
> Cheap grace means the justification of sin without the justification of the sinner. . . . Cheap grace is not the kind of forgiveness of sin which frees us from the toils of sin. Cheap grace is the grace we bestow on ourselves.[6]

More recently, another Evangelical minister has grown weary of what he has come to call "easy-believism." He has written:

> The more I have examined Jesus' public ministry and His dealings
> with inquirers, the more apprehensive I have become about the
> methods and content of contemporary evangelism. On a disturbing
> number of fronts, the message being proclaimed today is not the
> gospel according to Jesus.
>
> The gospel in vogue today holds forth a false hope to sinners. It
> promises them they can have eternal life yet continue to live in rebel-
> lion against God. Indeed, it encourages people to claim Jesus as Savior
> yet defer until later the commitment to obey Him as Lord. It promises
> salvation from hell but not necessarily freedom from iniquity. It offers
> false security to people who revel in the sins of the flesh and spurn the
> way of holiness. By separating faith from faithfulness, it leaves the
> impression that intellectual assent is as valid as wholehearted obedience
> to the truth. Thus the good news of Christ has given way to the bad
> news of an insidious easy-believism that makes no moral demands on
> the lives of sinners. It is not the same message Jesus proclaimed.

"This new gospel," the writer continues, "has spawned a generation of professing Christians whose behavior often is indistinguish-
able from the rebellion of the unregenerate." Thus, he concludes,

> We have no business preaching grace to people who do not under-
> stand the implications of God's law. It is meaningless to expound on
> grace to someone who does not know the divine demand for righ-
> teousness. Mercy cannot be understood without a corresponding
> understanding of one's own guilt. A gospel of grace cannot be
> preached to someone who has not heard that God requires obedience
> and punishes disobedience.[7]

As we shall see, the grace of God, provided through the intercession of the Savior, is free yet expensive; it is costly grace, "costly
because it costs a man his life, and it is grace because it gives a man
the only true life. . . . Above all, it is costly because it cost God the
life of his Son . . . and what has cost God much cannot be cheap for
us. Above all, it is grace because God did not reckon his Son too dear
a price to pay for our life, but delivered him up for us."[8] Far too
many "assume that because Scripture contrasts faith and works, faith
may be devoid of works. They set up a concept of faith that eliminates
submission, yieldedness, or turning from sin, and they categorize all
the practical elements of salvation as human works. They stumble

over the twin truths that salvation is a gift, yet it costs everything."[9]

With the restoration of the gospel through the Prophet Joseph Smith have come vital verities relative to this matter of grace and works, sacred truths that help to establish the essential but delicate balance between what God has done and what we must do.

Paul and James on Abraham: Grace and Works

One of the major theological challenges in the Christian world for centuries has been what appeared to be the apparent contradiction between the writings of Paul and the epistle of James. As we have noted above, Paul places great stress upon the need for trusting and relying wholly upon the merits of Jesus Christ and thus of accepting the gifts of grace offered through him. James, on the other hand, devotes a substantial portion of his general letter to expounding the point that "faith without works is dead." James's stress upon the necessity for works led Martin Luther to call the epistle of James "an epistle of straw" and to propose that it be deleted from the scriptural canon on the basis that it contradicted the pure gospel taught by Paul to the Christian communities of the first century.

Indeed, without the elevated and clarifying perspective provided by the Book of Mormon, modern revelation, and latter-day prophets, we would be at a loss to understand what is involved and what was intended by these two mighty servants of the Lord. In Romans 4, Paul essentially asks the question, "What was it that made Abraham such a great man? Why was he accepted of the Lord?" The answer is very simple, Paul suggests: Abraham had faith—believed God—and it was accounted unto him for righteousness. In James 2, the brother of the Lord essentially asks, "What was it that made Abraham such a great man? Why was he accepted of the Lord?" It could not have been his faith alone, James suggests. No, he contends, Abraham's faith was manifest and evident in his willingness to sacrifice his son Isaac—in his works.

In reality, it was Abraham's faith that brought the approbation of God. And it was Abraham's works that brought forth the blessings of heaven. President Joseph Fielding Smith explained:

> Paul taught these people—who thought that they could be saved by some power that was within them, or by observing the law of

Moses—he pointed out to them the fact that if it were not for the mission of Jesus Christ, if it were not for this great atoning sacrifice, they could not be redeemed. And therefore it was by the grace of God that they are saved, not by any work on their part, for they were absolutely helpless. Paul was absolutely right.

And on the other hand, James taught just as the Lord taught, just as Paul had taught in other scripture, that it is our duty, of necessity, to labor, to strive in diligence, and faith, keeping the commandments of the Lord, if we would obtain that inheritance which is promised to the faithful, and which shall be given unto them through their faithfulness to the end. There is no conflict in the doctrines of these two men.[10]

Necessary and Sufficient Conditions

As we have seen already, the grace of God is a *necessary* condition for salvation; there is no way, in time or in eternity, that man could produce the plan of salvation—create himself, fall, or redeem himself—for such is the work of the Gods. But the grace of God is a gift to mankind, a gift which must be perceived and received to be efficacious. The works of man—the ordinances of salvation, the deeds of service and acts of charity and mercy—are *necessary* for salvation; they evidence man's commitment and fulfill his covenant with Christ to do all in his power to live the life of a Saint and overcome the world, even as he who is our prototype did. But the works of man will never be enough to qualify one for the eternal prize; acting alone, without the grace and mercy and condescension of God, these deeds are but paltry offerings and are thus not *sufficient* for salvation. And thus it is that Moroni, at the end of the Nephite record, invited us to "come unto Christ, and be perfected in him, and deny yourselves of all ungodliness; and if ye shall deny yourselves of all ungodliness, and love God with all your might, mind and strength, *then is his grace sufficient for you,* that by his grace ye may be perfect in Christ" (Moroni 10:32, italics added).

Elder Orson Pratt provided an excellent summary of the principle we are here considering.

> We are to understand from [Ephesians 2:8-10], that the grace and faith by which man is saved, are the gifts of God, having been purchased for him not by his own works, but by the blood of Christ. Had not these gifts been purchased for man, all exertions on his part would

have been entirely unavailing and fruitless. Whatever course man might have pursued, he could not have atoned for one sin; it required the sacrifice of a sinless and pure Being in order to purchase the gifts of faith, repentance, and salvation for fallen man. Grace, Faith, Repentance, and Salvation, when considered in their origin, are not of man, neither by his works; man did not devise, originate, nor adopt them; superior Beings in Celestial abodes, provided these gifts, and revealed the conditions to man by which he might become a partaker of them. Therefore all boasting on the part of man [Ephesians 2:9] is excluded. He is saved by a plan which his works did not originate—a plan of heaven, and not of earth.

Well might the Apostle declare to the Ephesians, that these gifts were not of themselves, neither of their works, when the God and Father of our spirits, from whom cometh every good and perfect gift, was the great Author of them. But are these great gifts bestowed on fallen man without his works? No: man has these gifts purchased for and offered to him; but before he can receive and enjoy them he must exercise his agency and accept of them: and herein is the condemnation of man, because when he was in a helpless fallen condition, and could not by his own works and devices atone for the least of his sins, the Only Begotten of the Father gave his own life to purchase the gifts of faith and salvation for him, and yet he will not so much as accept of them.[11]

After All We Can Do

In short, "however good a person's works, he could not be saved had Jesus not died for his and everyone else's sins. And however powerful the saving grace of Christ, it brings exaltation to no man who does not comply with the works of the gospel."[12] Or to echo the glorious words of Nephi, we encourage all "to believe in Christ, and to be reconciled to God; for *we know that it is by grace that we are saved, after all we can do*" (2 Nephi 25:23, italics added; compare 10:24). There has been, unfortunately, some confusion about this phrase. Some Latter-day Saints have supposed that the grace of Christ is not available to us until *after*, meaning following the time, we have done everything we can do. Who among us has done everything? All of us fall short of the ideal. Further, the grace of Christ is not just the final boost into celestial glory provided by a merciful Lord, although we will need a full measure of enabling power to qualify for exaltation. Rather, grace is God presently at work in our lives. In short, we don't need to wait until the Judgment to be assisted and empowered; thankfully, the Lord helps us all along the way.

No more heinous doctrine could exist than that which encourages lip service to God but discourages wholehearted obedience and the works attendant to discipleship. And surely no more diabolical belief could exist than that which encourages the kind of smug self-assurance that comes from trusting in one's own works, relying upon one's own strength, and seeking to prosper through one's own genius. It is an affront to God and a mock of the atoning power of him whom God sent, for man to place himself at the center of things, for him to revel in his own greatness and marvel at his own achievements. Pure humanism is a doctrine of the devil: it places an inordinate emphasis upon fallible man and thus deflects man's vision away from the heavens and the powers of redemption. Even among some Latter-day Saints we frequently find that an overemphasis upon man as "a god in embryo" tends to underplay the effects of the Fall and thus the constant need for divine assistance in overcoming the natural man (see Mosiah 3:19). The key to understanding this sacred principle—the relationship between the grace of a perfect, infinite God and the works of an imperfect, finite man—is balance, balance and perspective provided through the scriptures of the Restoration and the words of living oracles of this dispensation.

Conclusion

Glenn L. Pearson offered an analogy that might prove helpful in understanding the balance we have been discussing.

> A man is wandering in a hot and barren waste, and about to die of thirst, when he is caused to look up at the top of the hill where he sees a fountain of water in a restful setting of green grass and trees. His first impulse is to dismiss it as a mirage sent to torture his weary soul. But, being wracked with thirst and fatigue, and doomed to certain destruction anyway, he chooses to believe and pursue this last hope. As he drives his weary flesh to the top of the hill, he begins to see evidence of the reality of his hope; and, renewing his efforts, struggles on to the summit where he wets his parched lips, cools his fevered brow, and restores life to his body as he drinks deeply from the fountain. He is saved!
>
> What saved him? Was it the climb up the hill? Or was it the water?

If he had remained at the foot of the hill either because of disbelief or lack of fortitude, his only means of salvation would have remained inaccessible. On the other hand, if he had climbed to the top and found he had labored in vain, he would have been worse off, if possible. . . .

The climb up the hill represents obedience to the gospel (faith in Christ, repentance, baptism of water, baptism of the Spirit, and endurance to the end); the water is that same eternal drink which Jesus offered the woman at the well. It is the atonement of Christ which is supplied as an act of grace.[13]

President Harold B. Lee wisely taught: "Spiritual certainty that is necessary to salvation must be preceded by a maximum of individual effort. Grace, or the free gift of the Lord's atoning power, must be preceded by personal striving."[14] Or, in the words of Paul, "Ye are justified of faith and works, through grace, to the end the promise might be sure to all the seed; not to them only who are of the law, but to them also who are of the faith of Abraham; who is the father of us all" (JST, Romans 4:16).

Notes

1. Kenneth L. Woodward, "What Mormons Believe," *Newsweek,* 1 September 1980, p. 68, italics added.

2. See *Teachings of the Prophet Joseph Smith,* sel. Joseph Fielding Smith (Salt Lake City: Deseret Book Co., 1976), p. 121.

3. Cited in Bruce C. Hafen, *The Broken Heart* (Salt Lake City: Deseret Book Co., 1989), pp. 2-3.

4. "What Think Ye of Salvation by Grace?" *1983-84 Fireside and Devotional Speeches* (Provo, Utah: Brigham Young University Press, 1984), pp. 47-48.

5. From Roland Bainton, *Here I Stand* (New York: Mentor, 1950), pp. 49-50.

6. Dietrich Bonhoeffer, *The Cost of Discipleship* (New York: Macmillan, 1963), pp. 45, 46, 47.

7. John F. MacArthur, Jr., *The Gospel According to Jesus* (Grand Rapids, Michigan: Zondervan, 1988), pp. 15-16, 85.

8. Bonhoeffer, *The Cost of Discipleship,* pp. 47-48.

9. MacArthur, *The Gospel According to Jesus,* p. 31.

10. *Doctrines of Salvation,* comp. Bruce R. McConkie, 3 vols. (Salt Lake City: Bookcraft, 1954-56), 2:310.

11. From N. B. Lundwall, comp., *A Compilation Containing the Lectures on Faith . . . Also a Treatise on True Faith by Orson Pratt. . . .* (Salt Lake City: Bookcraft, n. d.), pp. 82-83.

12. Spencer W. Kimball, *The Teachings of Spencer W. Kimball,* ed. Edward L. Kimball (Salt Lake City: Bookcraft, 1980), p. 71.

13. *Know Your Religion* (Salt Lake City: Bookcraft, 1961), pp. 92-93.

14. *Stand Ye in Holy Places* (Salt Lake City: Deseret Book Co., 1974), p. 213.

If their works were good in this life,
and the desires of their hearts were good, . . .
they should also, at the last day,
be restored unto that which is good.
—Alma 41:3

16

The Desires of Our Hearts

*B*y 1831 the headquarters of the restored Church had moved from New York and Pennsylvania to Ohio. In late 1832 the Lord gave instructions for the establishment of a "school of the prophets," calling specifically for "a house of prayer, a house of fasting, a house of faith, a house of learning, a house of glory, a house of order, a house of God" (D&C 88:119).

The course of study and pondering and prayer and faith of the School of the Prophets anticipated temple worship and proved to be a pattern for how all of the Saints were to come before the Lord in sacred places in all holiness of heart. The God of ancient Israel gave particular direction to modern Israel that a temple was to be erected, "in the which house," the Lord Jehovah explained, "I design to endow those whom I have chosen with power from on high" (D&C 95:8). The Saints came to know that if they would give their all in sacrifice—would provide whatever time and talents and means were required—for the building of the temple, the heavens would be opened and their labors would be rewarded. The Saints were obedient and the word of God was verified. There followed, especially in early 1836, a pentecostal season, an era of unusual spiritual enlightenment and refreshment.

Alvin Smith: A Scriptural Prototype

The leadership of the Church had begun meeting in the Kirtland Temple even before it was completed. On Thursday, 21 January 1836, the First Presidency, the high councils from Ohio and Missouri, and the patriarch of the Church, Joseph Smith, Sr., were engaged in a series of meetings. In the evening the Prophet took part in what came to be known as a "blessing meeting," an occasion on which priesthood blessings were bestowed and prophetic utterances made.

After the presidency had laid their hands upon Joseph Smith's head and pronounced many blessings, the Prophet was taken into vision. "The heavens were opened upon us, and I beheld the celestial kingdom of God, and the glory thereof" (D&C 137:1). The Prophet described the "transcendent beauty" and grandeur of that holy abode, including the wondrous glory of the throne of God and the streets of that kingdom. He saw Adam and Abraham there. He also saw his mother and father, indicating that the vision was a glimpse into a future celestial world, inasmuch as both parents were still alive; Father Smith was, of course, in the same room with the Prophet. (D&C 137:2-5.) And then Joseph saw in vision "my brother Alvin, that has long since slept; and marveled how it was that he had obtained an inheritance in that [celestial] kingdom, seeing that he had departed this life before the Lord had set his hand to gather Israel the second time, and had not been baptized for the remission of sins" (D&C 137:5-6).

Alvin Smith, the oldest of Joseph and Lucy Mack Smith's children, was born in 1798. He was a noble soul, a sensitive young man solicitous of others' needs, particularly his parents'. He became seriously ill on 15 November 1823 from what Mother Smith called a "bilious colic," probably what we would know today as appendicitis. An experimental drug, calomel, was administered by a local physician. The calomel "lodged in his stomach," according to Lucy, and Alvin began to die of gangrene. He passed away on 19 November, and a pall of gloom and sorrow spread beyond the Smith home to the entire neighborhood.

Inasmuch as Alvin had died some seven years before the formal organization of the Church (and thus had not been baptized by proper authority), Joseph wondered how it was possible for Alvin to have attained the highest heaven. Alvin's family had been shocked and saddened at his funeral when they heard the Presbyterian minister announce that Alvin would be consigned to hell, having never officially been baptized or involved in the church. What joy and excitement must have filled the souls of both Joseph, Jr. and Joseph, Sr. as they learned a comforting truth from an omniscient and omniloving God: "Thus came the voice of the Lord unto me, saying: All who have died without a knowledge of this gospel, who would have received it if they had been permitted to tarry, shall be heirs of the celestial kingdom of God; also, all that shall die henceforth without a knowledge of it, who would have received it with all their hearts, shall be heirs of that kingdom; for I, the Lord, will judge all men according to their works, according to the desire of their hearts" (D&C 137:7-9).

God does not and will not hold anyone accountable for a gospel law of which he or she was ignorant. Every person will have opportunity—here or hereafter—to accept and apply the principles of the gospel of Jesus Christ. Only the Lord, the Holy One of Israel, is capable of "keeping the gate" and thus discerning completely the hearts and minds of mortal men; he alone knows when a person has received sufficient knowledge or impressions to constitute a valid opportunity to receive the gospel message. Joseph had reaffirmed that the Lord will judge men not only by their actions, but also by their attitudes—the desires of their hearts.

Alma explained to an errant son:

It is requisite with the justice of God that men should be judged according to their works; and if their works were good in this life, *and the desires of their hearts were good*, that they should also, at the last day, be restored unto that which is good.

And if their works are evil they shall be restored unto them for evil. Therefore, all things shall be restored to their proper order, every thing to its natural frame—mortality raised to immortality, corruption to incorruption—raised to endless happiness to inherit the kingdom of God, or to endless misery to inherit the kingdom of the devil, the one on one hand, the other on the other—

The one raised to happiness according to his desires for happiness, or good according to his desires of good; and the other to evil according to his desires of evil; for as he has desired to do evil all the day long even so shall he have his reward of evil when the night cometh. (Alma 41:3-5, italics added; compare 29:4.)

One of the gracious acts of an omniscient Lord is his willingness to reward our righteous desires as well as our deeds. Alvin Smith is our scriptural prototype, the classic illustration of a righteous soul who was prohibited, because of circumstances beyond his control, from partaking fully of gospel blessings. Elder Dallin H. Oaks has described this glorious principle as follows:

> Just as we will be accountable for our evil desires, we will also be rewarded for our righteous ones. Our Father in Heaven will receive a truly righteous desire as a substitute for actions that are genuinely impossible. My father-in-law was fond of expressing his version of this principle. When someone wanted to do something for him but was prevented by circumstances, he would say: "Thank you. I will take the good will for the deed."
>
> This is the principle that blessed Abraham for his willingness to sacrifice his son Isaac. The Lord stopped him at the last instant (see Genesis 22:11-12), but his willingness to follow the Lord's command "was accounted unto him for righteousness" (D&C 132:36).
>
> This principle means that *when we have done all that we can, our desires will carry us the rest of the way. It also means that if our desires are right, we can be forgiven for the unintended errors or mistakes we will inevitably make as we try to carry those desires into effect.* What a comfort for our feelings of inadequacy![1]

To those who had not been overly endowed with this world's goods, King Benjamin spoke of their duty to the beggar: "I say unto the poor, ye who have not and yet have sufficient, that ye remain from day to day; I mean all you who deny the beggar, because ye have not; I would that ye say in your hearts that: I give not because I have not, but if I had I would give. And now, if ye say this in your hearts ye remain guiltless." (Mosiah 4:24-25.) As opposed to our legal systems in society that could never punish or reward according to motive alone, "the laws of God can reward a righteous desire or attitude because an omniscient God can determine it. If a person does not perform a particular commandment because he is genuinely unable to do so, but truly would if he could, our Heavenly Father will know this and will reward that person accordingly."[2]

The implications of this divine principle are especially comforting for those who seek an interest in the kingdom of God, all who aspire to holiness, who yearn to go where God is and be as he is but who wrestle with the foibles and weaknesses of a fallen world. We are able to "come boldly unto the throne of grace" (Hebrews 4:16; see also Moses 7:59), to approach the Father in the name of the Son, knowing that the God of grace will receive of our righteous desires as an acceptable offering. The brother of Jared thus presented himself before the Lord with his sixteen transparent stones to receive heavenly assistance. "O Lord," he prayed, "thou hast said that we must be encompassed about by the floods. Now behold, O Lord, and do not be angry with thy servant because of his weakness before thee; for we know that thou art holy and dwellest in the heavens, and that we are unworthy before thee; because of the fall our natures have become evil continually; nevertheless, O Lord, thou hast given us a commandment that we must call upon thee, that from thee we may receive according to our desires" (Ether 3:2).

Fruit of the Spirit

The grace of the Lord Jesus is manifest not only in his mercy to us—in his willingness to receive of and judge us according to our desires as well as our works—but also in bringing about the kinds of changes in our nature that result in additional works of righteousness. That is to say, through a power beyond ourselves we begin to perform the labors and deeds that evidence a clean heart. In the world there are "works of the flesh"—immorality, witchcraft, murder, hatred, strife, and sedition; but within the community of believers there is "fruit of the Spirit," the godly walk and conversation that bear witness of Christ's power to renew and transform humanity. "The fruit of the Spirit"—the works that flow naturally from a regenerated heart—"is love, joy, peace, long-suffering, gentleness, goodness, faith, meekness, temperance: against such there is no law. And they that are Christ's have crucified the flesh with the affections and lusts. If we live in the Spirit, let us also walk in the Spirit." (Galatians 5:19-25.)

Likewise King Benjamin spoke of the manner in which the Saint—the member of Christ's church who has begun to retain a remission of sins from day to day and to grow in the knowledge and glory of God—conducts his or her life. We note that the following are not commandments and directives from a priesthood leader as

much as they are descriptions of how the Saints act, how the fruit of
the Spirit flows from the lives of the faithful.

> And ye will not have a mind to injure one another, but to live
> peaceably, and to render to every man according to that which is his
> due.
> And ye will not suffer your children that they go hungry, or naked;
> neither will ye suffer that they transgress the laws of God, and fight
> and quarrel one with another, and serve the devil. . . .
> But ye will teach them to walk in the ways of truth and soberness;
> ye will teach them to love one another, and to serve one another.
> And also, ye yourselves will succor those that stand in need of your
> succor; ye will administer of your substance unto him that standeth in
> need; and ye will not suffer that the beggar putteth up his petition to
> you in vain, and turn him out to perish. (Mosiah 4:13-16.)

C. S. Lewis remarked that "if conversion to Christianity make no
improvement in a man's outward actions—if he continues to be just
as snobbish or spiteful or envious or ambitious as he was before—
then I think we must suspect that his 'conversion' was largely imagi-
nary. . . ."

> Fine feelings, new insights, greater interest in "religion" mean
> nothing unless they make our actual behaviour better; just as in an ill-
> ness "feeling better" is not much good if the thermometer shows that
> your temperature is still going up. In that sense the outer world is
> quite right to judge Christianity by its results. Christ told us to judge
> by results. A tree is known by its fruit; or, as we say, the proof of the
> pudding is in the eating.

If "what we are," Lewis observed, "matters even more than what
we do—if, indeed, what we do matters chiefly as evidence of what we
are—then it follows that the change which I most need to undergo is
a change that my own direct, voluntary efforts cannot bring about.
. . . I cannot, by direct moral effort, give myself new motives. . . . We
realize that everything which really needs to be done in our souls can
be done only by God."[3]

Conclusion

Man may look upon the outward appearance, but God looks upon the heart (1 Samuel 16:7), upon the desires, upon the inner yearnings and silent pleadings of the soul. He not only sees all we do, but he knows all we feel and all we are. There is great comfort in knowing that the Lord can both perceive and purify our feelings, can both recognize and renew the desires of our hearts. Truly God "looketh down upon all the children of men; and he knows all the thoughts and intents of the heart; for by his hand were they all created from the beginning" (Alma 18:32; compare D&C 6:16).

Notes

1. *Pure in Heart* (Salt Lake City: Bookcraft, 1988), p. 59, italics added.

2. Dallin H. Oaks, *Pure in Heart*, pp. 12-13.

3. *Mere Christianity* (New York: Macmillan, 1952), pp. 165, 175-76.

Yea, come unto Christ, and be perfected in him,
and deny yourselves of all ungodliness.
—Moroni 10:32

17

Perfection by the Grace of Christ

*J*esus' call to a higher righteousness, embodied in that masterful discourse we know as the Sermon on the Mount, contained the penetrating and poignant statute: "Ye are therefore commanded to be perfect, even as your Father who is in heaven is perfect" (JST, Matthew 5:50). Many months later that same Lord, now resurrected and glorified, commanded his Saints in the western hemisphere, "Therefore I would that ye should be perfect even as I, or your Father who is in heaven is perfect" (3 Nephi 12:48).

This commandment to be perfect, to conform absolutely to the laws and ordinances of the gospel, did not, however, originate with Christ in the meridian of time. As Jehovah he had spoken in those terms to Abraham, the father of the faithful: "And when Abram was ninety years old and nine, the Lord appeared to Abram, and said unto him, I am the Almighty God, walk before me, and be thou perfect" (Genesis 17:1). Similarly, Jehovah commanded ancient Israel: "Thou shalt be perfect with the Lord thy God" (Deuteronomy 18:13). The directive has been given, the standard set. Nothing short of the ideal can possibly suffice: a being of absolute perfection could ask nothing less of his people.

Perfect in Our Generation

Addressing this subject, Elder Bruce R. McConkie wrote:

> *Perfection* is of two kinds—*finite or mortal,* and *infinite or eternal.*
> *Finite perfection* may be gained by the righteous saints in this life. It
> consists in living a God-fearing life of devotion to the truth, of walking
> in complete submission to the will of the Lord, and of putting first in
> one's life the things of the kingdom of God. *Infinite perfection* is
> reserved for those who overcome all things and inherit the fulness of
> the Father in the mansions hereafter. It consists in gaining eternal life,
> the kind of life which God has in the highest heaven within the celes-
> tial world.[1]

In one sense, to be perfect is to be complete, whole, mature, fully
focused. Only Jesus of Nazareth maintained a perfect walk in this life
in the sense that he navigated the strait and narrow path without
moral detour or transgression; he alone achieved moral perfection
and completed mortality without flaw or error. But others have
achieved perfection in the sense that they did all that was commanded
them, in the sense that they gave themselves wholly to the accom-
plishment of the will of the Lord. The scriptural record attests that
"Noah found grace in the eyes of the Lord; for Noah was a just man,
and perfect in his generation; and he walked with God, as did also his
three sons, Shem, Ham, and Japheth" (Moses 8:27; compare Genesis
6:9). The same is said of Seth, the son of Adam (see D&C 107:43).
Further, "there was a man in the land of Uz, whose name was Job;
and that man was perfect and upright, and one that feared God, and
eschewed evil" (Job 1:1).

What do the scriptures mean when they speak of a person being
"perfect in his generation"? President Brigham Young explained that
"we all occupy diversified stations in the world and in the kingdom of
God."

> Those who do right, and seek the glory of the Father in heaven,
> whether they can do little or much, if they do the very best they know
> how, they are perfect. . . . "Be ye as perfect as ye can," for that is all we
> can do tho it is written, "Be ye perfect as your Father who is in heaven
> is perfect." To be as perfect as we possibly can according to our knowl-
> edge is to be just as perfect as our Father in Heaven is. He cannot be
> any more perfect than he knows how, any more than we. When we are
> doing as well as we know in the sphere and station which we occupy
> here we are justified. . . . We are as justified as the angels who are
> before the throne of God.[2]

We can, therefore, attain unto finite perfection, through divine assistance—through grace—in this life; that is to say, we can become *perfect in our generation,* even as were Seth and Noah and Job and all of the faithful Saints of ages past.

Means to Perfection

A careful search of holy writ affirms that there are certain activities, certain labors, that move man toward finite perfection in this life and on toward that perfection that prevails among the Gods hereafter. Paul explained that the Church of Jesus Christ—the organization, offices, councils, and ordinances—had been established "for the perfecting of the saints, for the work of the ministry, for the edifying of the body of Christ" (Ephesians 4:12; see also JST, Hebrews 6:1-2). Paul wrote to Timothy that "all Scripture given by inspiration of God, is profitable for doctrine, for reproof, for correction, for instruction in righteousness: that the man of God may be perfect, thoroughly furnished unto all good works" (JST, 2 Timothy 3:16-17). Paul also taught that those who have gone before us—who were denied access to the gospel covenant because it was unavailable to them—cannot be made perfect without us, without our vicarious assistance; neither can we be made perfect without the appropriate ties between ancestry and posterity, between roots and branches (see Hebrews 11:40; D&C 128:15). Finally, the prophets and Apostles have repeatedly declared that patience (James 1:4) and suffering (Hebrews 2:10; 5:8; JST, Hebrews 11:40; 1 Peter 5:10) mold men and women toward that perfection that allows them to feel confidence in the presence of him who is the embodiment of all that is whole and complete and perfect.

Perfection and Divine Intervention

As it is with being justified, and as it is with being sanctified, perfection is both a process and a condition. But whether we speak of a person being "perfect in his generation" or of that ultimate perfection that comes in and after the resurrection, we speak of something that is brought to pass only through the intervention of God. Man cannot justify himself. He cannot sanctify himself. And he certainly cannot perfect himself. The transformations from a fallen nature to a spiritual nature, from worldliness to holiness, from corruption to incorruption, and from imperfection to perfection are accomplished because divine powers bring them to pass. They are acts of grace.

The Apostle Paul wrote to the early Christians: "Now the God of peace, that brought again from the dead our Lord Jesus, that great shepherd of the sheep, through the blood of the everlasting covenant, make you perfect in every good work to do his will, working in you that which is well pleasing in his sight, through Jesus Christ; to whom be glory for ever and ever" (Hebrews 13:20-21). The chief Apostle warned the Saints late in the first century: "Be sober, be vigilant; because your adversary the devil, as a roaring lion, walketh about, seeking whom he may devour: whom resist steadfast in the faith, knowing that the same afflictions are accomplished in your brethren that are in the world. But the God of all grace, who hath called us unto his eternal glory by Christ Jesus, after that ye have suffered a while, make you perfect, stablish, strengthen, settle you." (1 Peter 5:8-10.) More specifically, people are made "perfect in Christ Jesus" (Colossians 1:28); they are "just men made perfect through Jesus the mediator of the new covenant, who wrought out this perfect atonement through the shedding of his own blood" (D&C 76:69).

Because God works upon the human soul to bring about perfection; because Deity has clearly in mind what must be done to achieve this lofty end; because the Lord knows us infinitely better than we know ourselves—for these reasons we do well to turn our lives over to him and trust in his purposes as well as his work schedule. "We may be content," C. S. Lewis has written, "to remain what we call 'ordinary people': but he [God] is determined to carry out a quite different plan."

> . . . On the one hand we must never imagine that our own unaided efforts can be relied on to carry us through the next twenty-four hours as "decent people." If He does not support us, not one of us is safe from some gross sin. On the other hand, no possible degree of holiness or heroism which has ever been recorded of the greatest saints is beyond what He is determined to produce in every one of us in the end. *The job will not be completed in this life; but He means to get us as far as possible before death. . . .*
>
> I find I must borrow . . . [a] parable from George MacDonald. Imagine yourself as a living house. God comes in to rebuild that house. At first, perhaps, you can understand what He is doing. He is getting

the drains right and stopping the leaks in the roof and so on: you knew that those jobs needed doing and so you are not surprised. But presently He starts knocking the house about in a way that hurts abominably and does not seem to make sense. What on earth is He up to? The explanation is that He is building quite a different house from the one you thought of—throwing out a new wing here, putting on an extra floor there, running up towers, making courtyards. You thought you were going to be made into a decent little cottage: but He is building a palace. He intends to come and live in it Himself.

The command "Be ye perfect" is not idealistic gas. Nor is it a command to do the impossible. He is going to make us into creatures that can obey that command. He said (in the Bible) that we were "gods" and He is going to make good His words. If we let Him—for we can prevent Him, if we choose—*He will make the feeblest and filthiest of us into a god or goddess,* dazzling, radiant, immortal creature, pulsating all through with such energy and joy and wisdom and love as we cannot now imagine, a bright stainless mirror which reflects back to God perfectly (though, of course, on a smaller scale) His own boundless power and delight and goodness. The process will be long and in parts very painful; but that is what we are in for. Nothing less. He meant what He said.[3]

The Process of Perfection

"The path of the just," a wise man has written, "is as the shining light, that shineth more and more unto the perfect day" (Proverbs 4:18). More fully, "That which is of God is light; and he that receiveth light, and continueth in God, receiveth more light; and that light groweth brighter and brighter until the perfect day" (D&C 50:24). That is to say, we begin the process of perfection in this life, we hold to the rod of iron through fidelity and devotion to the word of truth, and we continue through the veil of death into the world to come. There we continue in our same course—loving truth, seeking light, and cherishing virtue—until in and after the resurrection, "the perfect day," we gain that perfection that characterizes those who are exalted. Concerning the process of purification and perfection a modern revelation counseled the first elders of this dispensation as follows:

And again, verily I say unto you that it is your privilege, and a promise I give unto you that have been ordained unto this ministry, that inasmuch as you strip ̀yourselves from jealousies and fears, and humble yourselves before me, for ye are not sufficiently humble, the veil shall be rent and you shall see me and know that I am—not with the carnal neither natural mind, but with the spiritual.

For no man has seen God at any time in the flesh, except quickened by the Spirit of God.

Neither can any natural man abide the presence of God, neither after the carnal mind.

Ye are not able to abide the presence of God now, neither the ministering of angels; wherefore, *continue in patience until ye are perfected.* (D&C 67:10-13, italics added.)

We are never justified in lowering the lofty standard held out to followers of the Christ. Nor are our actions or attitudes approved of God if we suggest that the Savior did not mean what he said when he called us to the transcendent level of perfection. Our task is not to water down the ideal, nor to dilute the directive. Rather, we must view our challenge with perspective, must see things as they really are, but also as they really can be. "Pursuing the standard of perfection," one religious leader has observed, "does not mean that we can never fail. It means that when we fail we deal with it. Those with true faith will fail—and in some cases, frequently—but a genuine believer will, as a pattern of life, confess his sin and come to the Father for forgiveness (1 John 1:9). *Perfection* is the standard; *direction* is the test."[4]

Elder Bruce R. McConkie spoke on a number of occasions about the process of becoming perfect, of the necessity of Latter-day Saints exercising faith and having hope in Christ, and of pursuing the gospel course in a sane, balanced, and confident manner. "We don't need to get a complex or get feeling that you have to be perfect to be saved," he said to institute students in Salt Lake City. "You don't . . . have to live a life that's truer than true. You don't have to have an excessive zeal that becomes fanatical and becomes unbalancing. What you have to do is stay in the mainstream of the Church and live as upright and decent people live in the Church—keeping the commandments, paying your tithing, serving in the organizations of the Church, loving the Lord, staying on the strait and narrow path."[5] To Brigham Young University students Elder McConkie stated: "We have to become perfect to be saved in the celestial kingdom. But nobody becomes perfect in this life. Only the Lord Jesus attained that state, and he had an advantage that none of us has. He was the Son of God, and he came into this life with a spiritual capacity and a talent and an inheritance that exceeded beyond all comprehension what any of the rest of us was born with. . . ."

No other mortal—not the greatest prophets nor the mightiest apostles nor any of the righteous saints of any of the ages—has ever been perfect, but we must become perfect to gain a celestial inheritance. As it is with being born again, and as it is with sanctifying our souls, so becoming perfect in Christ is a process.

We begin to keep the commandments today, and we keep more of them tomorrow, and we go from grace to grace, up the steps of the ladder, and we thus improve and perfect our souls. . . .

As members of the Church, if we chart a course leading to eternal life; if we begin the processes of spiritual rebirth, and are going in the right direction; if we chart a course of sanctifying our souls, and degree by degree are going in that direction; and if we chart a course of becoming perfect, and, step by step and phase by phase, are perfecting our souls by overcoming the world, then it is absolutely guaranteed—there is no question whatever about it—we shall gain eternal life. Even though we have spiritual rebirth ahead of us, perfection ahead of us, the full degree of sanctification ahead of us, if we chart a course and follow it to the best of our ability in this life, then when we go out of this life we'll continue in exactly the same course. We'll no longer be subject to the passions and appetites of the flesh. We will have passed successfully the tests of this mortal probation and in due course we'll get the fulness of our Father's kingdom—and that means eternal life in his everlasting presence.

The Prophet told us that there are many things that people have to do, even after the grave, to work out their salvation. We're not going to be perfect the minute we die. But if we've charted a course, if our desires are right, if our appetites are curtailed and bridled, and if we believe in the Lord and are doing to the very best of our abilities what we ought to do, we'll go on to everlasting salvation, which is the fulness of eternal reward in our Father's kingdom.[6]

Conclusion

The children of the promise should and must have hope. "And what is it that ye shall hope for? Behold I say unto you that ye shall have hope through the atonement of Christ and the power of his resurrection, to be raised unto life eternal, and this because of your faith in him according to the promise." (Moroni 7:40-41.) Thus it is that Moroni extended the tender and timeless invitation to the Saints of God:

> Yea, come unto Christ, and be perfected in him, and deny your-selves of all ungodliness; and if ye shall deny yourselves of all ungodli-ness, and love God with all your might, mind, and strength, then is his grace sufficient for you, that by his grace ye may be perfect in Christ; and if by the grace of God ye are perfect in Christ, ye can in nowise deny the power of God.
>
> And again, if ye by the grace of God are perfect in Christ, and deny not his power, then are ye sanctified in Christ by the grace of God, through the shedding of the blood of Christ, which is in the covenant of the Father unto the remission of your sins, that ye become holy, without spot. (Moroni 10:32-33.)

The destination or condition of complete perfection may be some distance away, but through the aid of him who is full of grace and truth, as well as through our quiet perseverance, the journey can be both meaningful and inspiring. In the language of the Prophet Joseph Smith, "Happiness is the object and design of our existence; and will be the end thereof, if we pursue the path that leads to it; and this path is virtue, uprightness, faithfulness, holiness, and keeping all the commandments of God."[7] Further, President Spencer W. Kimball has declared, "the kind of life which brings happiness, brings also growth and development and leads toward perfection. Perfection is our goal, for with perfection comes exaltation and eternal life."[8]

Notes

1. *Mormon Doctrine*, 2d ed. (Salt Lake City: Bookcraft, 1966), p. 567, italics in original.

2. *Deseret News Weekly*, 31 August 1854, p. 37.

3. *Mere Christianity* (New York: Macmillan, 1952), pp. 173-74, italics added.

4. John F. MacArthur, Jr., *The Gospel According to Jesus* (Grand Rapids, Michigan: Zondervan, 1988), p. 192, italics in original.

5. "The Probationary Test of Mortality," Address to the institute of

religion students, University of Utah, 10 January 1982, p. 11.

6. "Jesus Christ and Him Crucified," *1976 Devotional Speeches of the Year* (Provo, Utah: Brigham Young University Press, 1977), pp. 399-401.

7. *Teachings of the Prophet Joseph Smith*, sel. Joseph Fielding Smith (Salt Lake City: Deseret Book Co., 1976), pp. 255-56.

8. *The Teachings of Spencer W. Kimball*, ed. Edward L. Kimball (Salt Lake City: Bookcraft, 1980), p. 156.

I am the vine, ye are the branches. . . .
Without me ye can do nothing.
—John 15:5

18

The True Vine and
the Branches

aith in Jesus Christ is the first principle of revealed religion. He is the foundation upon which we build our testimonies and the rock upon which any divine domicile is established. Helaman pleaded with his sons, Nephi and Lehi: "And now, my sons, remember, remember that it is upon the rock of our Redeemer, who is Christ, the Son of God, that ye must build your foundation; that when the devil shall send forth his mighty winds, yea, his shafts in the whirlwind, yea, when all his hail and his mighty storm shall beat upon you, it shall have no power over you to drag you down to the gulf of misery and endless wo, because of the rock upon which ye are built, which is a sure foundation, a foundation whereon if men build they cannot fall" (Helaman 5:12).

Power in the Person

To Christ we turn in the hour of need; he is the balm of Gilead. Upon him and his word we may rely with unshaken confidence; he is true and faithful. From him we can receive the realization of our fondest dreams; his name is Eternal, and the life we may enjoy with him is called Eternal Life.

To have faith in the name of Christ is to have an assurance, born of the Spirit, of our Lord's divine sonship, to know by revelation that no earthly man or woman—no matter how gifted and no matter how noble—could have done what He did. His work was and is the work of a God, and the product of his labors—salvation itself —is available only because of the merciful intercession of one with power over life and death.

To have faith in the name of Christ is to acknowledge his hand in all things, to confess that there are labors beyond the power of man to perform. Man cannot forgive his own sins any more than he can create himself. Man cannot cleanse and renew and regenerate the human soul any more than he can resurrect himself. These are the infinite actions of a God, and they require the intervention of godly powers in man's behalf. To have faith in the name of Christ is to recognize and receive the saving grace of Christ.

The power unto life and salvation is in Jesus Christ, the person. The power is not in programs, even inspired programs. Programs cannot save. They have not the power to forgive sins or sanctify or soothe troubled souls. It is the gospel of Jesus Christ that is "the power of God unto salvation" (Romans 1:16), a power that derives from him who is omnipotent. The Saints of all ages come to know by revelation the source of their salvation. Christianity without the living Christ is at best deficient. Righteousness without the Righteous One cannot redeem. Theology without the gospel lacks the power of salvation.

The Book of Mormon, which is another testament of Jesus Christ, provides a powerful pattern for members of the Church who seek deliverance from human suffering and spiritual sickness; it contains numerous illustrations of persons from the past who knew well where to turn in times of need. For example, after the people of King Benjamin had heard their prophet-leader's moving witness of the coming of the Lord God Omnipotent, they fell to the earth, "for the fear of the Lord had come upon them. And they had viewed themselves in their own carnal state, even less than the dust of the earth. And they all cried aloud with one voice, saying: O have mercy, and apply the atoning blood of Christ that we may receive forgiveness of our sins, and our hearts may be purified; for we believe in Jesus Christ, the Son of God, who created heaven and earth, and all things; who shall come down among the children of men."

We note with interest where their thoughts and their hearts were focused; we note that the center of their repentance was Jesus Christ, the person. And now we note from the account the results of their soul cries: "And it came to pass that after they had spoken these words the Spirit of the Lord came upon them, and they were filled with joy, having received a remission of their sins, and having peace of conscience, because of the exceeding faith which they had in Jesus Christ who should come." (Mosiah 4:1-3.) As the scriptures and the Apostles and prophets have always testified, the Lord's Church is an inspired and necessary vehicle; the system and organization and format for involvement in the work of the Church are divinely designed means to an end. But the Savior is the End, that toward which all things point and from which all things receive efficacy, virtue, and force here and hereafter.

Let us ponder upon the significance of another scriptural illustration. The prayers of a righteous father and a concerned community of believers in behalf of a wayward son called forth the intervention of heaven; Alma the Younger and the sons of Mosiah were struck down by an angel as they went about seeking to wreak havoc in the Nephite Church of Christ. Concerning the awful agonies of Alma's period of suffering and repentance and self-confrontation, he later explained in vivid detail: "I was racked with eternal torment, for my soul was harrowed up to the greatest degree and racked with all my sins. Yea, I did remember all my sins and iniquities, for which I was tormented with the pains of hell; yea, I saw that I had rebelled against my God, and that I had not kept his holy commandments. . . . The very thought of coming into the presence of my God did rack my soul with inexpressible horror."

Alma described the dramatic manner in which his soul was turned from poignant pain to perfect peace: "And it came to pass that as I was thus racked with torment, while I was harrowed up by the memory of my many sins, behold, I remembered also to have heard my father prophesy unto the people concerning the coming of one Jesus Christ, a Son of God, to atone for the sins of the world. Now, as my mind caught hold upon this thought, I cried within my heart: O Jesus, thou Son of God, have mercy on me, who am in the gall of bitterness, and am encircled about by the everlasting chains of death."

Again we attend with interest to the results of such pleadings—a sincere turn to Jesus Christ for deliverance—as contained in Alma's words: "And now, behold, when I thought this, I could remember my pains no more; yea, I was harrowed up by the memory of my sins no more. And oh, what joy, and what marvelous light I did behold; yea, my soul was filled with joy as exceeding as was my pain!" (Alma 36:12-20.)

In another instance the prophet Abinadi delivered a scathing denunciation of Noah and his priests, particularly of the manner in which they feigned allegiance to the law of Moses but failed to live in harmony with its moral precepts. Further, he corrected their false impression that salvation could come by the law alone. "I say unto you," he declared, "that it is expedient that ye should keep the law of Moses as yet; but I say unto you, that the time shall come when it shall no more be expedient to keep the law of Moses. And moreover, I say unto you, that salvation doth not come by the law alone; and were it not for the atonement, which God himself shall make for the sins and iniquities of his people, that they must unavoidably perish, notwithstanding the law of Moses." (Mosiah 13:27-28.)

Elder Bruce R. McConkie suggested a latter-day application of Abinadi's words:

> Suppose we have the scriptures, the gospel, the priesthood, the Church, the ordinances, the organization, even the keys of the kingdom—everything that now is down to the last jot and tittle—and yet there is no atonement of Christ. What then? Can we be saved?
>
> Will all our good works save us? Will we be rewarded for all our righteousness?
>
> Most assuredly we will not. We are not saved by works alone, no matter how good; we are saved because God sent his Son to shed his blood in Gethsemane and on Calvary that all through him might ransomed be. We are saved by the blood of Christ.
>
> To paraphrase Abinadi: "Salvation doth not come by the church alone: and were it not for the atonement, given by the grace of God as a free gift, all men must unavoidably perish, and this notwithstanding the Church and all that appertains to it."[1]

The True Vine

One of the most meaningful allegories in scripture is recorded by John. Jesus said to the Twelve: "I am the true vine, and my Father is the husbandman. Every branch in me that beareth not fruit he taketh away; and every branch that beareth fruit, he purgeth it, that it may bring forth more fruit. Now ye are clean through the word which I have spoken unto you. Abide in me, and I in you. As the branch cannot bear fruit of itself, except it abide in the vine; no more can ye, except ye abide in me. I am the vine, ye are the branches: He that abideth in me, and I in him, the same bringeth forth much fruit: for without me ye can do nothing." (John 15:1-5.)

In offering helpful commentary upon these verses, one New Testament scholar has written:

> The part of the Father here is decisive. He watches over the vine and takes action like that of a vine-dresser to secure fruitfulness. Every fruitless branch he takes away. . . . Left to itself a vine will produce a good deal of unproductive growth. For maximum fruitfulness extensive pruning is essential. This is a suggestive figure for the Christian life. The fruit of Christian service is never the result of allowing the natural energies and inclinations to run riot. . . . The man who so abides in Christ and has Christ abide in him keeps on bearing fruit in quantity. And the verse [verse 5] concludes with an emphatic declaration of human helplessness apart from Christ. In isolation from Him no spiritual achievement is possible.[2]

In short, "as long as the spiritual union between Christ and the believer, which (ideally and normally, at any rate) begins with Baptism, is maintained by faith, love, and prayer, the believer's soul is nourished by constant supplies of grace, just as truly as the branches of a vine are nourished by the sap that flows into them from the stem. Nourished by the life of Christ, the believer's soul is cleansed, sanctified, and made fruitful in all good works."[3] Those branches, on the other hand, that fail to acknowledge the source of their existence, that sever themselves from the mother vine or tree, that refuse pruning and refinement, never gain the strength or power to develop the fruit that remains (see John 15:16).

The Book of Mormon prophets spoke often of branches of Israel being "grafted" into the mother tree. This figurative expression finds meaning only in Christ, who is the Holy One of Israel, the God of Abraham, Isaac, and Israel. Indeed, the restoration of Israel is first and foremost a restoration to Jesus the Christ (Mormon 9:36). "After the house of Israel should be scattered," Nephi wrote, "they should be gathered together again; or, in fine, after the Gentiles had received the fulness of the Gospel, the natural branches of the olive-tree, or the remnants of the house of Israel, should be grafted in, or come to the knowledge of the true Messiah, their Lord and their Redeemer" (1 Nephi 10:14). Nephi later explained to his questioning brothers:

> And now, the thing which our father meaneth concerning the grafting in of the natural branches through the fulness of the Gentiles, is, that in the latter days, when our seed shall have dwindled in unbelief, yea, for the space of many years, and many generations after the Messiah shall be manifested in body unto the children of men, then shall the fulness of the gospel of the Messiah come unto the Gentiles, and from the Gentiles unto the remnant of our seed.
>
> And at that day shall the remnant of our seed know that they are of the house of Israel, and that they are the covenant people of the Lord; and then shall they know and come to the knowledge of their forefathers, and also to the knowledge of the gospel of their Redeemer, . . . and the very points of his doctrine, *that they may know how to come unto him and be saved.*
>
> And then at that day will they not rejoice and give praise unto their everlasting God, their rock and their salvation? Yea, at that day *will they not receive the strength and nourishment from the true vine?* Yea, will they not come unto the true fold of God? (1 Nephi 15:13-15, italics added; compare Alma 16:13-17.)

Limits of Self-Reliance

We must do all that we can do. We must extend ourselves to the limit, must stretch and bend the soul to its extremities. In the final analysis, however—at least when dealing with matters pertaining to spiritual growth and progression—it is not possible to "pull ourselves up by our own bootstraps," nor is it healthy to presume we can. "By His grace," President Ezra Taft Benson explained, "and by our faith in [Christ's] atonement and our repentance of our sins, we receive the strength to do the necessary works that we otherwise could not do by our own power. By His grace, we receive an endowment of blessing and spiritual strength that may eventually lead us to eternal life if we endure to the end. By His grace, we become more like His divine personality."[4] With a deemphasis upon God, often there follows an overemphasis on man—his own abilities, his own strengths, his own potential. Such a humanistic view of man is accurately reflected in the now-famous poem by William Ernest Henley, "Invictus":

Out of the night that covers me,
    Black as the Pit from pole to pole,
I thank whatever Gods may be
    For my unconquerable soul.

In the fell clutch of circumstance
    I have not winced nor cried aloud.
Under the bludgeonings of chance
    My head is bloody, but unbowed.

Beyond this place of wrath and tears
    Looms but the Horror of the shade,
And yet the menace of the years
    Finds, and shall find me unafraid.

It matters not how strait the gate,
    How charged with punishments the scroll,
I am the master of my fate;
    I am the captain of my soul.

Elder Orson F. Whitney, a great Apostle-poet, responded to Henley as follows:

Art thou in truth? Then what of him
    Who bought thee with his blood?
Who plunged into devouring seas
    And snatched thee from the flood?

Who bore for all our fallen race
    What none but him could bear,
The God who died that man might live,
    And endless glory share?

Of what avail thy vaunted strength,
    Apart from his vast might?
Pray that his Light may pierce the gloom,
    That thou mayest see aright.

Men are as bubbles on the wave,
    As leaves upon the tree.
Thou, captain of thy soul, forsooth!
    Who gave that place to thee?

Free will is thine—free agency,
    To wield for right or wrong;

> But thou must answer unto him
>   To whom all souls belong.
>
> Bend to the dust that head "unbowed,"
>   Small part of Life's great whole!
> And see in him, and him alone,
>   The Captain of thy soul.[5]

Jesus Christ is the light and the life of the world (see Mosiah 16:9; Alma 38:9; 3 Nephi 11:10-11). In him and in him alone is to be found the abundant life (John 10:10). Christ seeks to reconcile finite men with their infinite Heavenly Father. He is Mediator, Intercessor, and Redeemer. In him is the power that may be extended to fallen men and women to become the sons and daughters of God, the means whereby we may resume, through appropriate reconciliation, our status in the royal family of God (John 1:11-12; D&C 34:1-4).

Conclusion

We believe in Christ, not because we can see him, but because through him we are able to see all other things with such crystal clarity. As we come to view Christ as he is, we also come to view ourselves in proper perspective. In fact, the more a person devotes himself to the Lord and keeps an eye single to His glory, the more he sees that Christ is able to make of him so much more than he could make of himself with his own limited and faltering resources. "The more we get what we now call 'ourselves' out of the way," C. S. Lewis reminds us, "and let Him take us over, the more truly ourselves we become. . . ."

> I am not, in my natural state, nearly so much of a person as I like to believe: most of what I call 'me' can be very easily explained. It is when I turn to Christ, when I give myself up to His Personality, that I first begin to have a real personality of my own. . . . Nothing that you have not given away will ever be really yours. Nothing in you that has not died will ever be raised from the dead. Look for yourself, and you will find in the long run only hatred, loneliness, despair, rage, ruin, and decay. But look for Christ and you will find Him, and with Him everything else thrown in.[6]

If our gaze is upon the Savior, we need look nowhere else. If our trust is in him and his word, we need pay little heed to the discordant voices all about us. The invitation and challenge is ever before us: "Look unto me in every thought; doubt not, fear not" (D&C 6:36).

Notes

1. "What Think Ye of Salvation by Grace?" *1983-84 Fireside and Devotional Speeches* (Provo, Utah: Brigham Young University Press, 1984), p. 48.

2. Leon Morris, *The Gospel According to John* (William B. Eerdmans Publishing Co., 1971), pp. 669, 671.

3. J. R. Dummelow, ed., *A Commentary on the Holy Bible* (New York: Macmillan, 1936), p. 800.

4. *Come Unto Christ* (Salt Lake City: Deseret Book Co., 1983), pp. 7-8.

5. *Improvement Era*, April 1926, p. 611.

6. *Mere Christianity* (New York: Macmillan, 1952), p. 15.

Praise ye the Lord.
Praise, O ye servants of the Lord,
praise the name of the Lord.
—Psalm 113:1

19

Singing the Song of Redeeming Love

*C*oming to know, as Moses did, "that man is nothing" (Moses 1:10) without the Lord—that we are, as Elder Orson F. Whitney observed, "as bubbles on the wave"—should create within each of us feelings not of futility but of reverent humility. We come in time to glory at the wonder and goodness and grace of our God. Indeed, how merciful he is to us!

His Yoke Is Easy

The Savior's gentle invitation to the burden-weary is touching and timeless: "Come unto me, all ye that labour and are heavy laden, and I will give you rest. Take my yoke upon you, and learn of me; for I am meek and lowly in heart: and ye shall find rest unto your souls. For my yoke is easy, and my burden is light." (Matthew 11:28-30.) One writer on the New Testament has provided the following insightful commentary upon the Lord's words:

> Jesus' hearers understood that the yoke was a symbol of submission. In the land of Israel yokes were made of wood, carefully fashioned by the carpenter's hand to fit the neck of the animal that was to wear it. Undoubtedly Jesus had made many yokes as a boy in Joseph's carpenter shop in Nazareth. This was a perfect illustration for salva-

tion. The yoke worn by the animal to pull a load was used by the master to direct the animal.

The yoke also signified discipleship. When our Lord added the phrase "and learn from Me," the imagery would have been familiar to Jewish listeners. In ancient writings, a pupil who submitted himself to a teacher was said to take the teacher's yoke. One writer records this proverb: "Put your neck under the yoke and let your soul receive instruction." Rabbis spoke of the yoke of instruction, the yoke of the Torah, and the yoke of the law. . . .

The yoke of the law, the yoke of human effort, the yoke of works, and the yoke of sin are all heavy, chafing, galling yokes. They represent large, unbearable burdens carried in the flesh. They lead to despair, frustration, and anxiety. Jesus offers a yoke we can carry, and He also gives the strength to carry it (cf. Philippians 4:13). Therein is true rest.

The yoke He offers is easy, and the burden He gives is light, because He is meek and lowly. Unlike the Pharisees and scribes, He does not desire to oppress us. He does not want to pile burdens on us we cannot bear, nor is He trying to show how hard righteousness can be. He is gentle. He is tender. And He gives a light burden to carry. Obedience under His yoke is a joy.[1]

It is true, writes Elder Neal A. Maxwell, that "to live so as to please Him is a rigorous undertaking. But His burden is light compared to the burdens of sin, insincerity, vanity, and hypocrisy. His burden is bearable because, once we shoulder it and it alone, we can, mercifully, leave so much else behind."[2]

The Master does not always remove every burden of life, every care, from our shoulders. Rather, he frequently provides for us that assistance, that strength—shall we call it grace? yes, for so it is—that allows us to bear up under what might otherwise be unbearable circumstances. For example, after Alma and his converts had fled the pestilential presence of Noah and his priests, they settled in a place which they named Helam. A Lamanite army soon overtook them, however, and Amulon, a vicious man—a former priest of Noah who knew and despised the righteous Alma—was placed at the head of the colony in Helam. "And now it came to pass that Amulon began to exercise authority over Alma and his brethren, and began to persecute him, and cause that his children should persecute their children. . . . He exercised authority over them, and put tasks upon them, and put taskmasters over them. And it came to pass that so great were their afflictions that they began to cry mightily to God." Amulon thereupon forbade the Nephites to pray and promised death to those who were caught in that act. How bitter is the irony that so many dissipate their energies in fighting a God whose existence they refuse to admit! Had Amulon not feared the God of Alma and his people, he would not have feared their prayers. The death ban on prayer is assuredly an admission on his part of the efficacy of prayer and the reality of Israel's God.

Alma and his people now began to cry to the Lord in their hearts. The God of mercy and grace heard their pleas for deliverance. "Lift up your heads," he said to them, "and be of good comfort, for I know of the covenant which ye have made unto me; and I will covenant with my people and deliver them out of bondage. And I will also ease the burdens which are put upon your shoulders, that even you cannot feel them upon your backs, even while you are in bondage."

Mormon's account of this wondrous occasion follows: "And now it came to pass that the burdens which were laid upon Alma and his brethren were made light; yea, the Lord did strengthen them that they could bear up their burdens with ease, and they did submit cheerfully and with patience to all the will of the Lord." (Mosiah 24:8-15.) Soon thereafter the Lord led Alma and his followers miraculously out of danger to the land of Zarahemla, where they joined the Saints under Mosiah.

The Song of Redeeming Love

In refocusing the minds of the Saints of his day upon their covenantal obligations and upon the spiritual experiences upon which those covenants were first made, Alma asked: "And now behold, I say unto you, my brethren, if ye have experienced a change of heart, and if ye have felt to sing the song of redeeming love, I would ask, can ye feel so now?" (Alma 5:26.)

Alma knew well the need for continuing spiritual refreshment, for constant and current renewal of faith, and for a growing and deepening commitment to and acknowledgment of the Almighty God. A testimony is a fragile possession, something that must be nurtured and fed and exercised. We seek to establish reservoirs of faith in our lives, ever-present sources of strength and encouragement in times of difficulty; at the same time, we cannot forever live in the past, cannot survive forevermore on memories, even on marvelous and meaningful memories. Alma's question, "If ye have felt to sing the song of redeeming love, . . . can ye feel so now?" gets at the heart of gospel living, at the foundation of Christlike service. One who is motivated by his love of the Lord, his sense of overwhelming gratitude for the Father and the Son, is prone to stay on course and seek that closeness with the Holy Spirit that will help him to retain a remission of sins from day to day (see Mosiah 4:11-12).

To sing the song of redeeming love is to joy in the matchless majesty of God's goodness, to know the wonder of God's love. It is to sense and know, by the power of the Holy Ghost, that the Lord is intimately involved with his children and that he cares, really cares, about their well-being; it is to relish and cherish the fruit that is the most joyous to the soul (see 1 Nephi 11:22-23). Jacob surely sang the song of redeeming love when he exulted in the wisdom of God, the greatness and justice of God, the mercy of God, the goodness of God, and the holiness of God (2 Nephi 9).

To sing the song of redeeming love is to experience that transcendent spiritual gift that the scriptures call charity, the pure love of Christ (see Moroni 7:47). It is to feel a driving sense of urgency to love and serve others purely, even as Christ does. But it is also to love Christ purely, to partake of a quality and depth of soul-love for him that knows no earthly or temporal counterparts. It is to love and honor and worship and praise the Lord as God with feelings and emotions that are unspeakable. Elder Melvin J. Ballard attempted to describe such an experience in the following words:

> I found myself one evening in the dreams of the night in that sacred building, the temple. After a season of prayer and rejoicing I was informed that I should have the privilege of entering into one of those rooms to meet a glorious Personage, and, as I entered the door, I saw, seated on a raised platform, the most glorious Being my eyes have ever beheld or that I ever conceived existed in all the eternal worlds. As I approached to be introduced, he arose and stepped towards me with extended arms, and he smiled as he softly spoke my name. If I shall live to be a million years old, I shall never forget that smile. He took me into his arms and kissed me, pressed me to his bosom, and blessed me, until the marrow of my bones seemed to melt! When he had finished, I fell at his feet, and, as I bathed them with my tears and kisses, I saw the prints of the nails in the feet of the Redeemer

of the world. The feeling that I had in the presence of Him who hath all things in His hands, to have His love, His affection, and His blessing was such that if I ever can receive that of which I had but a foretaste, I would give all that I am, all that I ever hope to be to feel what I then felt.[3]

Similarly, Elder George F. Richards sought to explain the ineffable sense of love and gratitude that one can feel for his Lord and Savior:

> More than forty years ago I had a dream which I am sure was from the Lord. In this dream I was in the presence of my Savior as he stood in mid-air. He spoke no word to me, but my love for him was such that I have not words to explain. I know that no mortal man can love the Lord as I experienced that love for the Savior unless God reveals it to him. I would have remained in his presence, but there was a power drawing me away from him.
>
> As a result of that dream, I had this feeling that no matter what might be required of my hands, what the gospel might entail unto me, I would do what I should be asked to do even to the laying down of my life.
>
> And so when we read in the scriptures what the Savior said to his disciples, "In my Father's house are many mansions: . . . I go to prepare a place for you . . . that where I am, there ye may be also" (John 14:2-3), I think that is where I want to be.
>
> If only I can be with my Savior and have that same sense of love that I had in that dream, it will be the goal of my existence, the desire of my life.[4]

It is not only those who have seen the Lord—have enjoyed a personal appearance, a dream, or a vision—who sing the song of redeeming love, but all those who have had the burdens of sin, the weight of guilt, and the agonies of bitterness, hostility, or pain removed by the Great Physician. They all shout praises to the Holy One of Israel. They all bow the knee in humble reverence and gratitude toward him who shall yet rule and reign as King of kings and Lord of lords. "Peace I leave with you," he said, "my peace I give unto you: not as the world giveth, give I unto you. Let not your heart be troubled, neither let it be afraid" (John 14:27). Only through Christ the Lord may mankind know "the peace of God, which passeth all understanding" (Philippians 4:7).

Hope in Christ

We must have hope. We must have rejoicing. If any people in all the wide world have reason to be positive, to rejoice and exult in blessings unmeasured and graces abounding, it is the Latter-day Saints. If any religious body in all of creation ever had reason to look forward to the future, to prepare with joyful anticipation for that which is yet to be, it is the members of the restored Church. I am convinced that much of the discouragement that exists in the hearts and minds of some Latter-day Saints may be traced to their inability to rely on the Lord and trust in his mercies. As stated again and again in this work, we need to do all we can to prove ourselves worthy of the Lord's goodness, to seek to live the life of a true Saint. But we must also come to know that when we have done all we can—when we have stretched to the limit, have placed our offerings upon the altar of faith, no matter how meager they may seem to us at the time—we then have done what was asked of us and the Lord is pleased with us. Thus we need to "distinguish more clearly between divine discontent and the devil's dissonance, between dissatisfaction with self and disdain for self. . . . We can contemplate how far we have already come in the climb along the pathway to perfection; it is usually much further than we acknowledge, and such reflections restore resolve. . . . We can allow for the reality that God is still more concerned with growth than with geography. . . . This is a gospel of grand expectations, but God's grace is sufficient for each of us if we remember that there are no instant Christians."[5]

Conclusion

We feel to sing praises to the King Emmanuel with a modern Apostle who penned the following fitting and appropriate psalm:

> Praise ye the Lord:
> Praise him for his goodness;
> Praise him for his grace;
> Exalt his name and seek his face—
> O praise ye the Lord.
>
> Blessed is the Lord:

Bless him for his mercy;
Bless him for his love;
Exalt his name and seek his face—
O blessed is the Lord.

Praise ye the Lord:
Praise him who all things did create;
Praise him who all things did redeem;
Exalt his name and seek his face—
O praise ye the Lord.

Seek ye the Lord:
Seek him who rules on high;
Seek him whose will we know;
Exalt his name and seek his face—
O seek ye the Lord.[6]

Notes

1. John F. MacArthur, Jr., *The Gospel According to Jesus* (Grand Rapids, Michigan: Zondervan, 1988), pp. 112-13.

2. *We Will Prove Them Herewith* (Salt Lake City: Deseret Book Co, 1982), p. 105.

3. *Melvin J. Ballard: Crusader for Righteousness* (Salt Lake City: Bookcraft, 1966), pp. 138-39.

4. Cited by Spencer W. Kimball in Conference Report, April 1974, pp. 173-74.

5. Neal A. Maxwell, *Notwithstanding My Weakness* (Salt Lake City: Deseret Book Co., 1981), pp. 9, 11.

6. Bruce R. McConkie, in Conference Report, October 1973, p. 57.

I am come that they might have life,
and that they might have it more abundantly.
—John 10:10

20

Life in Christ

$\mathcal{T}$he gospel of Jesus Christ has been restored to recreate the human family, to make available to fallen men and women those powers and attributes that will capacitate them for life with Christ, and to enable them to feel confidence in the presence of holy beings. The plan of salvation, what Joseph Smith called "the gospel of reconciliation,"[1] is the divine path by which man's relationship with the Father is reestablished and his place in the royal family secured. The gospel prepares men and women, not alone to be with their exalted Master but also to be as he is, so that "when he shall appear, we shall be like him" (1 John 3:2). The prophetic plea and invitation is thus forever the same: "I would that ye should come unto Christ, who is the Holy One of Israel, and partake of his salvation, and the power of his redemption. Yea, come unto him, and offer your whole souls as an offering unto him, and continue in fasting and praying, and endure to the end; and as the Lord liveth ye will be saved." (Omni 1:26.)

Putting Off the Natural Man

The angel explained to King Benjamin:

> Men drink damnation to their own souls except they humble themselves and become as little children, and believe that salvation was, and is, and is to come, in and through the atoning blood of Christ the Lord Omnipotent.

For the natural man is an enemy to God, and has been from the fall of Adam, and will be, forever and ever, unless he yields to the enticings of the Holy Spirit, and putteth off the natural man and becometh a saint through the atonement of Christ the Lord, and becometh as a child, submissive, meek, humble, patient, full of love, willing to submit to all things which the Lord seeth fit to inflict upon him, even as a child doth submit to his father. (Mosiah 3:18-19.)

One does not put off the natural man by simply living longer. He does not change his nature by simply attending meetings and being involved in the work of the Church, important as such activities are. Rather, after a person commits himself to a righteous life, the transformation from the natural state to the spiritual is accomplished through the mediation and atonement of Jesus Christ.

No person goes from death to life without that enabling power we call the grace of God. Programs to develop self-control, plans to modify human behavior, schemes bent on the shaping of more appropriate actions—these have fallen and will forever fall short of the mark that Christ has set. The first step to meaningful and permanent change is to focus one's attention upon and guide one's life by correct principles, to become grounded in truth. "True doctrine, understood," Elder Boyd K. Packer has taught, "changes attitudes and behavior. *The study of the doctrines of the gospel will improve behavior quicker than a study of behavior will improve behavior.* Preoccupation with unworthy behavior can lead to unworthy behavior. That is why we stress so forcefully the study of the doctrines of the gospel."[2]

Those who are born again or born from above—who die as to the things of unrighteousness and begin to live as pertaining to the things of the Spirit—are as little children. First and foremost, they are, like children, clean and pure. Through the atoning blood of Christ they have had their sins remitted and have entered the realm of divine experience. Putting off the natural man involves putting on Christ. As Paul counseled the Saints in his day, those who put off the old man are "renewed in the spirit of [their] mind." They "put on the new man, which after God is created in righteousness and true holiness." (Ephesians 4:22-24.) The "new man" is one who is "renewed in knowledge after the image of him that created him" (Colossians 3:8-10).

This renovation of the nature may for some be dramatic and rapid. Such was the case with Enos (Enos 1:1-8), with the people of

King Benjamin who underwent a "mighty change" (Mosiah 5:2), with Alma the Younger (Mosiah 27; Alma 36), and with Paul (Acts 9). As to the miraculous conversion of King Lamoni—and thus to the unspeakable power of Christ to forge new creatures—the Nephite record states:

> King Lamoni was under the power of God; [Ammon] knew that the dark veil of unbelief was being cast away from his mind, and the light which did light up his mind, which was the light of the glory of God, which was a marvelous light of his goodness—yea, this light had infused such joy into his soul, the cloud of darkness having been dispelled, and that the light of everlasting life was lit up in his soul, yea, he knew that this had overcome his natural frame, and he was carried away in God (Alma 19:6).

For others, the change the scriptures call the new birth may be less sudden, less dramatic. For example, the Savior, in speaking to the Nephites before his visit to them, said: "And ye shall offer for a sacrifice unto me a broken heart and a contrite spirit. And whoso cometh unto me with a broken heart and a contrite spirit, him will I baptize with fire and with the Holy Ghost, even as the Lamanites, because of their faith in me at the time of their conversion, were baptized with fire and with the Holy Ghost, and they knew it not" (3 Nephi 9:20). "We must be cautious," President Ezra Taft Benson has warned us, "as we discuss these remarkable examples. Though they are real and powerful, they are the exception more than the rule. For every Paul, for every Enos, and for every King Lamoni, there are hundreds and thousands of people who find the process of repentance much more subtle, much more imperceptible. Day by day they move closer to the Lord, little realizing they are building a godlike life."[3]

A vital part of putting off the natural man and becoming whole before God is an application of the grace of Christ, which enables the man of Christ to do more than theologize, more than sermonize on these matters. The gospel is more than systematic theology. It is more than a codification of intellectually stimulating doctrines. These things must become real, must become more than abstract metaphysical ideas. In the words of C. S. Lewis, the animation of human character "is precisely what Christianity is about. This world is a great sculptor's shop. We are the statues and there is a rumour going round the shop that some of us are some day going to come to life."[4]

To the degree that the attributes of godliness become a part of the disciple and are thereby reflected in his countenance and in his relationship with Deity, he is no longer a servant but is a son or daughter, and as such is an heir to the unspeakable blessings of the royal family (see Galatians 3-4). Having been born again into a new family relationship, he seeks thereafter to qualify for that consummation in mortality wherein he is sealed into the family of God. As King Benjamin implored: "I would that ye should be steadfast and immovable, always abounding in good works, that Christ, the Lord God Omnipotent, may seal you his, that you may be brought to heaven, that ye may have everlasting salvation and eternal life" (Mosiah 5:15).

Fruit of the Spirit

Those who have put off the natural man—what Paul called the "works of the flesh"—begin to enjoy what he called the "fruit of the Spirit," namely, "love, joy, peace, longsuffering, gentleness, goodness, faith, meekness, temperance"; they begin to "walk in the Spirit." (Galatians 5:19-25.) As Benjamin explained, such persons are humble and submissive, eager to know and carry out the will of the Savior, eager to have their own wishes swallowed up in the higher will of God. The Spirit of God sanctifies—it cleanses and purges filth and dross out of the human soul as though by fire. The Spirit does far more, however, than remove uncleanness. It also fills. It fills one with a holy element, with a sacred presence that motivates the person to a godly walk and goodly works. These persons do not necessarily plan out how they will perform the works of righteousness; they do not plot and design which deeds and what actions are to be done in every situation. Rather, they embody righteousness. They are goodness. In their lives, works are seldom a means to some end; good works flow from a regenerate heart and evidence their commitment to Christ. Yes, these persons do have agency. Indeed, they are free, because they have given themselves up to the Lord and his purposes. They choose to do good, but their choices are motivated by the Spirit of the Lord.

The work of the salvation of a soul thus consists of the union of that soul with Christ, a steady but powerful process by which the human and the mortal take on the powers and attributes of the infinite and the divine. But that is not all. Elder B. H. Roberts wrote:

This salvation from the effects of personal sins is not only a matter of forgiveness of past sins; a matter of justification before God; a matter of re-establishing union with God, which is spiritual life. It is a matter of sanctification of the soul; and of power to maintain the renewed spiritual life with God. It is a matter that involves human desires and human will. Surely it is unthinkable that God would hold man in union with himself against his desire, or against his will. Such a condition would not be "union" but bondage. The co-operation of man then in this work of his personal salvation becomes an absolute necessity.[5]

Paul wrote: "I am crucified with Christ: nevertheless I live; yet not I, but Christ liveth in me" (Galatians 2:20). A scripture that has caused no small stir among Latter-day Saint missionaries and their contacts but which teaches a profound lesson is: "For by grace are ye saved through faith; and that not of yourselves: it is the gift of God: not of works, lest any man should boast." And now note the following verse: "For we are his workmanship, created in Christ Jesus unto good works." (Ephesians 2:8-10.) One of the New Testament passages often quoted by Latter-day Saints—generally seeking to establish from scripture that men are not saved by grace alone—is the following, again from Paul: "Wherefore, my beloved, as ye have always obeyed, not as in my presence only, but now much more in my absence, work out your own salvation with fear and trembling." And how do we do this? The following verse explains: "For it is God which worketh in you both to will and to do of his good pleasure." (Philippians 2:12-13.)

In a revelation given at the time of the organization of the restored Church, the Lord warned a group of people who wanted to join the Church without receiving its baptism:

> Behold, I say unto you that all old covenants have I caused to be done away in this thing; and this is a new and an everlasting covenant, even that which was from the beginning.
>
> Wherefore, although a man should be baptized an hundred times it availeth him nothing, for you cannot enter in at the strait gate by the law of Moses, neither by your dead works.
>
> For it is because of your dead works that I have caused this last covenant and this church to be built up unto me, even as in days of old.

Wherefore, enter ye in at the gate, as I have commanded, and seek not to counsel your God. Amen. (D&C 22:1-4.)

Contextually, the term *dead works* in this revelation refers to baptisms performed in other churches which had not the authority from God to perform them. By extension, dead works could mean labors not grounded in faith, deeds and actions and covenants not performed in righteousness. For the purpose of our present discussion, dead works may also consist of works void of the motivation and staying power found in and through the Holy Ghost. Such an insight might provide a rather different (but meaningful) glimpse into the following from the Savior's Sermon on the Mount:

Verily I say unto you, it is not everyone that saith unto me, Lord, Lord, that shall enter into the kingdom of heaven; but he that doeth the will of my Father who is in heaven.

For the day soon cometh, that men shall come before me to judgment, to be judged according to their works.

And many will say unto me in that day, Lord, Lord, have we not prophesied in thy name; and in thy name cast out devils; and in thy name done many wonderful works?

And then will I say, Ye never knew me; depart from me ye that work iniquity. (JST, Matthew 7:30-33.)

Among his Nephite disciples the resurrected Lord explained that it is when a church is truly built upon his gospel (as well as called by his name) that it is his church. "And if it so be that the church is built upon my gospel then will the Father show forth his own works in it. But if it be not built upon my gospel, and is built upon the works of men, or upon the works of the devil, verily I say unto you they have joy in their works for a season, and by and by the end cometh, and they are hewn down and cast into the fire, from whence there is no return." (3 Nephi 27:10-11.)

Paul taught that whatever works are not of faith—are not motivated by one's faith in and dedication to Christ, works that are spiritually inert—are ultimately sin (Romans 14:23). On the other hand, those works that come—as does the fruit of the Spirit—by the power of the Holy Ghost, lift and lighten. They are deeds of faith and wonder which renew. Such works focus on and witness of Christ, who is their source; these good works are seen of men, that observers may glorify God (see Matthew 5:16). Such works are more than duty or assignment; they become liberating privileges and opportunities. Surely these are the kinds of labors to which the Master calls us when he says: "Come unto me, all ye that labour and are heavy laden, and I will give you rest. Take my yoke upon you, and learn of me; for I am meek and lowly in heart: and ye shall find rest unto your souls. For my yoke is easy, and my burden is light." (Matthew 11:28-30.)

Perhaps the highest and grandest fruit of the Spirit is love, what the scriptures call charity, the pure love of Christ (Moroni 7:47). "And again I remember," Moroni stated humbly to his Master, "that thou hast said that thou hast loved the world, even unto the laying down of thy life for the world. . . . And now I know that this love which thou hast had for the children of men is charity; wherefore, except men shall have charity they cannot inherit that place which thou hast prepared in the mansions of thy Father." (Ether 12:33-34.)

This love is more than an emotion, higher than a sweet feeling, more transcendent than a desire to perform good deeds. It is a fruit of the Spirit, a heavenly endowment that must be granted and bestowed by an all-loving God. It is this love that will prevent a multitude of sins (JST, 1 Peter 4:8). "Above all things," the Lord counseled the Saints in 1832, "clothe yourselves with the bond of charity, as with a mantle, which is the bond of perfectness and peace" (D&C 88:125; compare Colossians 3:14). It is this love that will shelter us from the storms of the day and cradle us in the midst of adversity or personal trial. Elder Jeffrey R. Holland has taught:

> Life has its share of some fear and some failure. Sometimes things fall short, don't quite measure up. Sometimes in both personal and public life, we are seemingly left without strength to go on. Sometimes people fail us, or economies and circumstance fail us, and life with its hardship and heartache can leave us feeling very alone.
>
> But when such difficult moments come to us, I testify that there is one thing which will never, ever fail us. One thing alone will stand the test of all time, of all tribulation, all trouble, and all transgression. One thing only never faileth—and that is the pure love of Christ. . . .
>
> . . . Only the pure love of Christ will see us through. It is Christ's love which suffereth long, and is kind. It is Christ's love which is not puffed up nor easily provoked. Only his pure love enables him—and us—to bear all things, believe all things, hope all things, and endure all things.[6]

To acquire and demonstrate that pure love from God is to have passed from death to life (1 John 3:14). When we have the Lord's love in our lives, our work in the Church becomes a labor of love; the keeping of God's statutes is no longer viewed or experienced as burdensome. "For this is the love of God," John wrote, "that we keep his commandments: and his commandments are not grievous" (1 John 5:3). And to keep the commandments is to be "in Christ" (see 1 John 2:5; 3:23-24; D&C 50:43).

Our Fundamental Duty

So where do we go from here? We have discussed the ideal. We have seen that the prophets and the Lord challenge us to strive for a higher righteousness, a new life, for that life which is in Christ Jesus. But what do we do? Of course we must strive to do what is right, even if our hearts have not been fully changed. Saints cannot remain stagnant. They cannot sit idly by while others perform the labors of the kingdom. They certainly are not justified in doing wrong because they are yet unclean. At the same time, our task is to seek regularly and consistently for that Spirit that gives life and light, and that gives substance and consequence to our deeds. Our task is not to run faster than we have strength, to labor harder than we have means, or to be truer than true. Our zeal for righteousness must always be tempered and appropriate and must be accompanied with wisdom. Zion is established in process of time (see Moses 7:21), and, with but few exceptions, the pure in heart become so in the same manner.

It would appear that the most fundamental and sacred assignment the Latter-day Saints have is to seek the Spirit, to pray for and live worthy of that spiritual influence, that revelatory and sanctifying power that is the rightful inheritance of baptized members of the Church. The role of the Holy Ghost is to lead men and women to the point of illumination and inspiration at which they are eventually ready to be ushered into the presence of the Father and the Son.

Joseph Smith taught—in paraphrasing the Savior—that the Holy Ghost "shall bring all things to remembrance, whatsoever things I have said unto you; *he shall teach you until ye come to me and my Father.*"[7] Before we attain to that transcendent privilege—either in this life or the next—and while we now labor, we are to cultivate the spirit of revelation and seek to be purified and filled by the Holy

Ghost. We seek first for the revealed witness of Christ, of Joseph Smith and the Restoration, and of the truthfulness of the work in which we are now engaged. We petition the Lord daily for his refining influence upon our souls and long for him to teach and educate our consciences, to attune us with the Infinite, to the end that we come in time to feel about things as he does. We plead with the Almighty regularly to deepen our commitment to truth and intensify our loyalty to him and to his anointed servants. We call upon the Father day by day to heighten our sensitivity to people, to their pains, their feelings, their desires, and to grant us a portion of his love in order that we can minister in his name and lift others through that sublime influence. And in the process we ever walk diligently but vigilantly, taking care that we do our duties in the Church, love and serve our fellowmen, and conduct ourselves with dignity and fidelity. We ask God to assist us in living a sane and balanced life, in living "by every word that proceedeth forth from the mouth of God" (D&C 84:44). In short, we seek the Spirit and strive with all our hearts to enjoy its sweet fruit and its marvelous privileges.

"Hereby know we that we dwell in him, and he in us, because he hath given us of his Spirit" (1 John 4:13). To have "the mind of Christ" (1 Corinthians 2:16) is to enjoy the promptings and guidance of the Spirit, to live in such a manner that our feelings, our desires, and our thoughts are receptive to divine direction. The modern Seer Joseph Smith taught the brethren of the School of the Prophets concerning the Eternal Godhead:

[Christ] received a fullness of the glory of the Father, possessing the same mind with the Father, which mind is the Holy Spirit, that bears record of the Father and the Son, and . . . these three constitute the Godhead, and are one; the Father and the Son possessing the same mind, the same wisdom, glory, power, and fullness—filling all in all. . . . [Christ is] filled with the fullness of the mind of the Father; or, in other words, the Spirit of the Father, which Spirit is shed forth upon all who believe on his name and keep his commandments; and all those who keep his commandments shall grow up from grace to grace, and become heirs of the heavenly kingdom, and joint heirs with Jesus Christ; possessing the same mind, being transformed into the same image or likeness, . . . and become one in [Christ], even as the Father, Son, and Holy Spirit are one.[8]

Conclusion

Jesus Christ is the Way, the Truth, and the Life; no person in all eternity will come unto Elohim the Father except by and through Jehovah the Son (John 14:6). The work of redemption, the preparation and ultimate creation of new beings, is the work of a God and thus is a labor that is infinite and eternal.

Joseph Smith wrote in 1834 that "darkness covers the earth, and gross darkness the minds of the inhabitants thereof . . . crimes of every description are increasing among men . . . intemperance, immorality, extravagance, pride, blindness of heart, idolatry, the loss of natural affection; the love of this world, and indifference toward the things of eternity increasing among those who profess a belief in the religion of heaven. . . . And in the midst of all this, the day of the Lord [is] fast approaching when none except those who have won the wedding garment will be permitted to eat and drink in the presence of the Bridegroom, the Prince of Peace!" Thus the Prophet described aptly the dilemma of the last days, the description of a world wandering in darkness.

What is the antidote for the illness, the prescription for a people who know not their God or his holy ways? The following surely is one of the finest statements in our literature regarding the power and grandeur of the gospel, the "glad tidings" that Christ has come and that salvation is available.

> Impressed with the truth of these facts what can be the feelings of those who have been partakers of the heavenly gift and have tasted the good word of God and the powers of the world to come? Who but those that can see the awful precipice upon which the world of mankind stands in this generation, can labor in the vineyard of the Lord without feeling a sense of the world's deplorable condition? Who but those who have duly considered the condescension of the Father of our spirits, in providing a sacrifice for His creatures, a plan of redemption, a power of atonement, a scheme of salvation, having as its great objects, the bringing of men back into the presence of the King of heaven, crowning them in the celestial glory, and making them heirs with the Son to that inheritance which is incorruptible, undefiled, and which fadeth not away—who but such can realize the importance of a perfect walk before all men, and a diligence in calling upon all men to

partake of these blessings? How indescribably glorious are these things to mankind! Of a truth they may be considered tidings of great joy to all people.[9]

Notes

1. *Teachings of the Prophet Joseph Smith,* sel. Joseph Fielding Smith (Salt Lake City: Deseret Book Co., 1976), p. 192.

2. In Conference Report, October 1986, p. 20, italics added.

3. "A Mighty Change of Heart," *Ensign,* October 1989, p. 5.

4. *Mere Christianity* (New York: Macmillan Publishing Company, 1960), p. 140.

5. *Seventy's Course in Theology: Fourth Year—The Atonement* (Dallas: Reprinted by S. K. Taylor Publishing Co., 1976), pp. 112-13.

6. In Conference Report, October 1989, pp. 32-33.

7. *The Words of Joseph Smith,* eds. Andrew F. Ehat and Lyndon W. Cook (Provo: Religious Studies Center, Brigham Young University, 1980), pp. 14-15, italics and modern punctuation added.

8. *Lectures on Faith* (Salt Lake City: Deseret Book Co., 1985), 5:2.

9. *Teachings of the Prophet Joseph Smith,* pp. 47-48.

For other foundation can no man lay
than that is laid, which is Jesus Christ.
—1 Corinthians 3:11

21

***

The Only Sure Foundation

A very old tradition among the Jews holds that during the early stages of construction of the second temple, the builders, by mistake, discarded the cornerstone. Centuries later, in the midst of a long day of debate, Jesus, seemingly drawing upon this tradition, spoke of the irony associated with ignoring or dismissing him and his message. "Did ye never read in the scriptures," he asked, "The stone which the builders rejected, the same is become the head of the corner: this is the Lord's doing, and it is marvelous in our eyes?" (Matthew 21:42; compare Psalm 118:22-23; Acts 4:11.)

Among the Nephites, Jacob prophesied: "I perceive by the workings of the Spirit which is in me, that by the stumbling of the Jews they will reject the stone upon which they might build and have safe foundation" (Jacob 4:15). Those who refuse to build upon the rock of our Redeemer unwittingly lay a foundation that is shallow and shoddy and shifting. Their houses of faith will eventually crumble, and great will be the fall thereof.

Well had Isaiah counseled Israel: "Sanctify the Lord of hosts himself; and let him be your fear, and let him be your dread. And he shall be for a sanctuary; but for [some] a stone of stumbling and for a rock of offence." (Isaiah 8:13-14.) The Master said in the meridian of time: "I am the stone, and those wicked ones reject me. I am the head of the corner. . . . Wherefore, on whomsoever this stone shall fall, it shall grind him to powder." (JST, Matthew 21:51-52, 54.) More specifically, Peter warned that "unto you therefore who believe,

[Christ] is precious; but unto them who are disobedient, who stumble at the word, through disobedience, whereunto they were appointed, [the Lord is] a stone of stumbling, and a rock of offence" (JST, 1 Peter 2:7). In reality, Jesus our Lord, as the chief cornerstone, is the foundation stone upon which the plan of salvation, the whole gospel structure, rests, as well as the topmost stone or capstone, by which the last tiers of the building will be linked together. Truly he is Alpha and Omega, the Beginning and the End, the First and the Last.

Building Our Lives on Christ

Just prior to his death, Helaman, grandson of Alma, delivered parting counsel to his own sons, Nephi and Lehi. Like all of his prophetic predecessors, he counseled them to keep the commandments of God; to be true to their sacred names, to honor those who had once borne those names; and to lay up for themselves treasures in heaven, to seek to qualify for that eternal inheritance that the scriptures call eternal life. "O remember, remember, my sons," he continued, "the words which king Benjamin spake to his people; yea, remember that there is no other way nor means whereby man can be saved, only through the atoning blood of Jesus Christ, who shall come; yea, remember that he cometh to redeem the world." Helaman reminded them of the words of Amulek—that Christ, having power from the Everlasting Father, will not come to save mankind in their sins but *from* their sins. The mighty prophet-father then voiced this divine directive:

> And now, my sons, remember, remember, that it is upon the rock of our Redeemer, who is Christ, the Son of God, that ye must build your foundation; that when the devil shall send forth his mighty winds, yea, his shafts in the whirlwind, yea, when all his hail and his mighty storm shall beat upon you, it shall have no power over you to drag you down to the gulf of misery and endless wo, because of the rock upon which ye are built, which is a sure foundation, a foundation whereon if men build they cannot fall. (Helaman 5:9, 12.)

Perhaps the supreme challenge of this life is to build our lives on Christ, to erect a house of faith, a divine domicile in which he and his Spirit would be pleased to dwell. There is safety from Satan and his minions only in Christ. There is security only in his word and through his infinite and eternal power.

How, then, do we build on Christ? In a day when the winds are blowing and the waves beating upon our ship, how do we navigate our course safely into the peaceful harbor? What must we do to have our Savior pilot us through life's tempestuous seas? Amidst the babble of voices—enticing voices that threaten to lead us into forbidden paths or which beckon us to labor in secondary causes—how do the Saints of the Most High know the Way, live the Truth, and gain that Abundant Life? The revelations offer us some simple suggestions:

1. *Accept and experience his healing grace.* This book has been written to testify of the power that is in Christ, power not only to create the worlds and divide the seas but also to still the storms of the human heart, to heal the pain of scarred and beaten souls. We must learn to trust in him more, in the arm of flesh less. We must learn to rely on him more, and on man-made solutions less. We must learn to surrender our burdens to him more. We must learn to work to our limits and then be willing to seek that grace or enabling power that will make up the difference, that sacred power that makes all the difference! As we noted in the previous chapter, a life in Christ is one devoted to the quest for heightened spirituality, imbued with yearnings for the revelatory and sanctifying influences of the Holy Ghost. The more we enjoy the influence of the Holy Spirit, the more that Spirit will certify of the divine sonship of Christ and, Liahona-like, point our minds and hearts to the words of Christ that can lead us into a far better land of promise (see Alma 37:44-45).

2. *Search his scriptures.* Holy writ has been preserved to bring us to Christ and to establish us upon his doctrine. The man or woman who is a serious student of the revelations, who seeks diligently to apply scriptural precepts and principles—he or she can more readily see the hand of God and can also discern the handiwork of Lucifer. Such a person is more equipped to sift and sort through the sordid and the spurious, more prepared to distinguish the divine from the diabolical, the sacred from the secular. Mormon explained that "whosoever will may lay hold upon the word of God, which is quick and powerful, which shall divide asunder all the cunning and the snares and the wiles of the devil, and lead the man of Christ in a strait and narrow course across that everlasting gulf of misery which is pre-

pared to engulf the wicked—and land their souls, yea, their immortal souls, at the right hand of God in the kingdom of heaven, to sit down with Abraham, and Isaac, and with Jacob, and with all our holy fathers, to go no more out" (Helaman 3:29-30).

The "man of Christ" or the "woman of Christ" is one who seeks to come unto Christ through searching the records of those who have known him best. Joseph Smith encouraged the Saints:

> Search the scriptures—search the revelations which we publish, and ask your Heavenly Father, in the name of His Son Jesus Christ, to manifest the truth unto you, and if you do it with an eye single to His glory nothing doubting, He will answer you by the power of His Holy Spirit. You will then know for yourselves and not for another. You will not then be dependent on man for the knowledge of God; nor will there be any room for speculation. No; for when men receive their instruction from Him that made them, they know how He will save them.[1]

Elder Bruce R. McConkie explained to Church leaders: "However talented men may be in administrative matters, however eloquent they may be in expressing their views; however learned they may be in worldly things—they will be denied the sweet whisperings of the Spirit that might have been theirs unless they pay the price of studying, pondering, and praying about the scriptures."[2]

3. *Teach his doctrine.* There is a supernal power that accompanies the plain and direct teaching of doctrine. The views and philosophies of men, even good men—no matter how pleasingly they are stated or how lofty and timely they may seem—simply cannot engage the soul in the way the doctrines of the gospel can. If we teach doctrine, and if we do so with the power and persuasion of the Holy Ghost, our listeners will be turned to Christ, will come to rely on his merits, and will find joy and peace here and eternal reward hereafter. Elder Bruce R. McConkie illustrated this principle with a parable:

> Hear now the parable of the unwise builder:
> A certain man inherited a choice piece of ground whereon to build a house to shelter his loved ones from the storms of the day and the cold of the night.
> He began his work with zeal and skill, using good materials, for the need was urgent.

But in his haste, and because he gave no heed to the principles of proper construction, he laid no foundation, but commencing immediately, he built the floor, and raised the walls, and began to cover them with a roof.

Then, to his sorrow, because his house had no foundation, it fell and became a heap of rubble, and those whom he loved had no shelter.

Verily, verily, I say unto you: A wise builder, when he buildeth an house, first layeth the foundation and then buildeth thereon.

Hear now the interpretation of the parable of the unwise builder:

A certain Church officer was called to build a house of faith and righteousness and salvation for the souls entrusted to his care. Knowing he had been called by inspiration and having great zeal, he hastened to strengthen and build up the programs of the Church without first laying the foundation of faith and testimony and conversion.

He spent his time on mechanics and means and programs and procedures and teaching leadership and never laid the great and eternal foundation upon which all things must rest in the Lord's house—the foundation of our theology and our doctrine.

Elder McConkie summarized: "The foundation upon which we build our whole church system is one of testimony and faith and conversion. It is our theology; it is the doctrine God has given us in this day; it is the restored and revealed principles of eternal truth—these are the things that give us the ability to operate our programs and build houses of salvation."[3]

4. *Sustain his servants and hearken to their words.* The Savior taught the Twelve in the meridian of time: "He that receiveth you receiveth me, and he that receiveth me receiveth him that sent me" (Matthew 10:40; compare D&C 84:36). To receive the Apostles meant to accept them as the mouthpiece of Deity, recognizing their voice as his voice and their authority as his authority. One certainly could not accept the Father while rejecting the Son, and one could not accept the Son while rejecting those he had commissioned to act in his name. A rejection of Peter, James, and John, or any of the Twelve, was at the same time a rejection of Christ.

It is just so in our day. "Whether by mine own voice," the Lord has warned, "or by the voice of my servants, it is the same" (D&C 1:38). "Whosoever receiveth my word receiveth me," the Lord said in 1837, "and whosoever receiveth me, receiveth those, the First Presidency, whom I have sent, whom I have made counselors for my name's sake unto you" (D&C 112:20). Conversely, Jesus told his disciples that "he that despiseth you despiseth me; and he that despiseth me despiseth him that sent me" (Luke 10:16). Elder Marvin J. Ashton stated this same principle in brief but bold language: "Any Church member not obedient to the leaders of this Church will not have the opportunity to be obedient to the promptings of the Lord."[4]

There are members who feel they can enjoy a relationship with the Lord independent of his Church, separate and apart from the organization established by revelation. There are even those who feel they can stay close to the Lord while they criticize or find fault with the Church and its leaders. These critics are wrong. They have been deceived. They are painfully mistaken and are walking in slippery paths. No person comes to the Master who does not acknowledge the mantle worn by his anointed. There is no power to be found in Him independent of his constituted priesthood authorities.

We be Abraham's children, the Jews said to Jove;
We shall follow our Father, inherit his trove.
But from Jesus our Lord came the stinging rebuke:
Ye are children of him, whom ye list to obey;
Were ye Abraham's seed, ye would walk in his path,
And escape the strong chains of the father of wrath.

We have Moses the seer, and the prophets of old;
All their words we shall treasure as silver and gold.
But from Jesus our Lord, came the sobering voice:
If to Moses ye turn, then give heed to his word;
Only then can ye hope for rewards of great worth,
For he spake of my coming and labors on earth.

We have Peter and Paul, in their steps let us trod;
So religionists say, as they worship their God.
But speaks He who is Lord of the living and dead:
In the hands of those prophets, those teachers and seers,
Who abide in your day have I given the keys;
Unto them ye must turn, the Eternal to please.[5]

Those who come into the Church with full purpose of heart "are no more strangers and foreigners, but fellowcitizens with the saints, and of the household of God; and are built upon the foundation of the apostles and prophets, Jesus Christ himself being the chief corner stone; in whom all the building fitly framed together groweth unto an holy temple in the Lord" (Ephesians 2:19-21).

5. *Be believing. Have hope.* Jesus Christ is the Hope of Israel. Peace in this life and glory hereafter come because of and through him. Hope in Christ burns brightly in the hearts of those who have learned to do their best and have then turned to the Almighty for assistance. Frustration and spiritual exhaustion eventually surround those who seek to do it themselves; feelings of helplessness and hopelessness come to shroud those who through pride or ignorance strive to gain eternal glory by their works alone.

Salvation, which is exaltation, which is eternal life, is a gift (D&C 6:13; 14:7). It is not something which can, strictly speaking, be earned. Rather, the scriptures speak of it as being *inherited.* It is, in fact, the rightful inheritance of those who have been cleansed and renewed and quickened by the blood of the Sinless One, through the power of the Holy Ghost. These are they who trust in him, who acknowledge and rely upon his mighty arm, who wisely allow the Lord of Sabaoth to fight their battles. "Fear not, little flock," the Good Shepherd has lovingly said; "do good; let earth and hell combine against you, for if ye are built upon my rock, they cannot prevail. Behold, I do not condemn you; go your ways and sin no more; perform with soberness the work which I have commanded you. Look unto me in every thought; doubt not, fear not." (D&C 6:34-36.)

A Note of Testimony

I have desired to share my feelings and my reflections upon what I believe to be the burden of all scripture in regard to the matter of being saved by the grace of Christ. Though I cannot speak for the Church, I do believe what I have written to be true and in harmony with the message of the standard works and the words of modern Apostles and prophets.

I love the Lord Jesus Christ. I know, by the power of the Holy Ghost, that he lives. I know, further, that the plan of salvation represents a gracious offering on the part of the Father, and that, as the angel taught King Benjamin, "salvation was, and is, and is to come, in and through the atoning blood of Christ, the Lord Omnipotent" (Mosiah 3:18). When I consider what love and infinite mercy is manifest by our Savior in offering himself as a sacrifice for sin, my soul wells up with deep appreciation for him who is Eternal, and my desire to express gratitude to him who bought us with his blood knows no bounds.

I know that Joseph Smith was called in this final dispensation of grace to reveal anew the Gods of heaven and to organize the Lord's Church, the church which administers his gospel. It is my testimony that The Church of Jesus Christ of Latter-day Saints is, in the language of the revelation, "the only true and living church upon the face of the whole earth" (D&C 1:30); that it is in the line of its duty and is led by prophets and Apostles called and anointed through the spirit of prophecy and revelation; and that this restored Church is the sole repository of those priesthood powers and saving truths which will allow men and women to come unto Christ and be saved in the highest heaven of the celestial world. Of these things I have no doubt.

After Jesus had preached "hard doctrine" at Capernaum, many of his followers were offended "and walked no more with him. Then said Jesus unto the twelve, Will ye also go away?" Simon Peter, the chief Apostle, answered, no doubt for all of his apostolic colleagues— and, for that matter, for all who love the Lord in all ages and know of his absolute necessity and indispensability in the plan of life and salvation. "Lord," he said, "to whom shall we go? thou hast the words of eternal life, and we believe and are sure that thou art that Christ, the Son of the living God." (John 6:66-69.)

So it was in the first century and so it is now and forevermore: Jesus Christ is the name and the power by which peace and happiness and salvation are to be obtained. On his mighty arm we rely. Because of who he is and what he has done, there is no obstacle to eternal life too great to overcome. Because of him, our minds are at peace. Our souls may rest.

Notes

1. *Teachings of the Prophet Joseph Smith,* sel. Joseph Fielding Smith (Salt Lake City: Deseret Book Co., 1976), pp. 11-12.

2. From an address at the Regional Representatives Seminar, 2 April

1982, typescript, p. 2; cited in *Sermons and Writings of Bruce R. McConkie*, ed. Mark L. McConkie (Salt Lake City: Bookcraft, 1998), p. 238.

3. From an address at the Regional Representatives Seminar, 3 April 1981, typescript, pp. 9-10; cited in *Sermons and Writings of Bruce R. McConkie*, pp. 226-27.

4. From Germany Area Conference Report, August 1973, p. 23.

5. Bruce R. McConkie, in Conference Report, April 1974, pp. 100-101.

Index